A Long Way From Henry Street

VOLUME 2

Stories Written by School Nurses

MacGILL

DISCOUNT MEDICAL AND SCHOOL NURSE SUPPLIES

Established 1904

1-800-323-2841 • www.macgill.com

Compiled and Edited by Melissa Birch and Nick Heidtbrink

Front Cover Art by Mike Schmidt

MacGill & Company
1000 North Lombard Road
Lombard, IL 60148
1-800-323-2841
www.macgill.com

ISBN 978-0-9744720-1-0

Contents

Introduction

At the end of the 19th century, the Lower East Side of New York City was an impoverished neighborhood with cramped living spaces—which translated to dismal public health conditions.

Lillian Wald, a student at the Women's Medical College of New York, refused to accept the living conditions of this neighborhood and set out on a lifelong mission to make healthcare services more accessible. Her vision of "public health nursing" led to the construction of the Henry Street Settlement, which provided health services to the people of New York's Lower East Side. Continuing her vision of public health, Wald placed a nurse from the Henry Street Settlement, Lina Rogers Struthers, at a public school to reduce absenteeism and the spread of communicable diseases among children. Struthers was so successful that the New York City Board of Health organized a public school nursing program, the first such service offered anywhere in the world.

Over one hundred years later, over 50,000 school nurses nationwide bring the same core values to their jobs as Struthers did in 1902. Since the days when Henry Street nurses tended to children's needs, however, much has changed. *A Long Way From Henry Street, Volume 2* brings light to the changing role of school nurses and the new challenges that face them in today's society.

The stories in this book were written by school nurses who work in a diverse range of environments. From small midwestern towns to large coastal cities—impoverished inner-city neighborhoods to wealthy suburbs—these stories focus on a wide range of challenges and experiences that school nurses encounter. There are stories that reveal how school nurses worked with healthcare providers to ensure that a child received accurate diagnosis and treatment, often bringing a family medical care that was otherwise unattainable. Other stories show how nurses were able to look beyond a child's physical pain and offer much needed emotional support and guidance. Stories that chronicle the typical chaotic day in the life of a school nurse are included as well as instances where school nurses helped students overcome personal trauma. Of course, no book focusing on school nursing would be complete without humorous stories. This book contains more than one story about the innocent behavior of children that will make you laugh.

We encourage you to pass this book on to those who may not be aware of the need for school nurses and the impact they have on children's health. There are still many who don't realize that our changing society has brought about a whole new job description for school nurses. An increasing number of kids go to school with chronic illnesses, significant handicaps, and troubled home lives. Caroline Champion, RN, MSN accurately describes the changing role of the school nurse in her story entitled *The Truth About Real School Nursing:* "A school nurse must be good at everything, not only emergency care, but also nursing assessment, chronic illness management, complex medical conditions, epidemiology, prevention, safety, teaching, screening, communicating, care management, policy development, grant-writing, employee health, community health, legal issues, politics, advocacy, care plan development, pharmacology, computer documentation, and now RTI, Response to Intervention."

A Long Way From Henry Street, Volume 2 is written by and about the caring and imaginative school nurses who devote their lives to keeping children healthy and happy.

Confidentiality

Great measures were taken to ensure that strict confidentiality is maintained in each of the stories included in this book. Stories were reviewed and given special attention if they revealed private information about any individual. The names of students, parents, physicians, and other parties have been changed or omitted in a vast majority of stories. Further, any references to the names of schools, streets, cities, and states were omitted when necessary. In some cases, the name of the author of a story was omitted to be certain that no correlation could be made between a student and a personal situation. In other instances, even despite the fact that real names were not used, the author and/or editors sought and received permission to print from individuals described in their story.

Request for Feedback

We hope you enjoy this collection of stories and appreciate any feedback you might have. Please send your comments via e-mail to macgill@macgill.com or by regular mail to MacGill & Company, 1000 North Lombard Road, Lombard, IL 60148.

Acknowledgements

MacGill & Company would like to thank all of the school nurses who took time out of their busy schedules to submit a story for inclusion in this book. The sheer number of submissions that we received outnumbered the amount of pages we were able to print, regretfully forcing us to leave out many excellent stories.

We would also like to express our gratitude to the Henry Street Settlement. The Henry Street Settlement is located in New York, NY. Its core mission is to challenge the effects of urban poverty by providing individuals and families with essential social and cultural services. More information regarding the Henry Street Settlement can be found at www.henrystreet.org.

I.

Advocating for Children's Health

"Nothing is more rewarding than to help a student get appropriate medical attention when it is needed."

–Janett Doile, RN

Ya Gotta Listen

By Janett Doile, RN

Bobby was beginning to come into the health office frequently, which was unusual for him. He was not a regular complainer, but recently he had been in weekly. His complaints were vague. One time he might report "not feeling well" and the next time he would say his stomach hurt. Each time I would assess him, but nothing specific would come to mind. He never had a fever, and his throat and ears always looked normal. No localized abdominal tenderness or rebound tenderness was observed.

He did not describe or exhibit any symptoms that would lead me to think of a specific problem. He was a well-nourished, normal looking teenage boy. He continued to come in periodically and each time I would assess him. I talked with his father, who was suspicious that his son just wanted to come home from school now that football season was over.

One morning Bobby came directly to my office upon arriving at school. He was complaining of a stomachache. Again, I ran through the usual checks. Bobby then told me his stomach had hurt a little at home when he first got up, but that it REALLY hurt when they drove over the railroad tracks on the way to school. That's when the light bulb went off for me. The description that the jarring had caused more pain led me to believe Bobby had appendicitis. I called his father, and instructed that he should seek medical attention for his son. Bobby was in surgery several hours later.

It is easy, especially with regular visitors, to miss important clues. When we listen and really hear what our students are telling us, the pathway to help will become visible. Nothing is more rewarding than to help a student get appropriate medical attention when it is needed.

Discipline

By Jill Vaughn, RN

I am an elementary school nurse in a school of just under five hundred children ranging from Pre-K to 5th grade. My 8-year-old twins, Alex and Alexis, attend the same school where I work. One spring day in 2010, my daughter Alexis' best friend, Courtney, came to me crying. She said her left thigh was hurting. After speaking with her for a short time, she started sobbing and told me that her mother beat her with a belt because she was late coming home from a friend's house the previous night. Courtney hugged me and cried, saying, "All I want is for my mom to stop hitting me." Courtney is mixed race and darker skinned so I was doubtful I would see any bruising on her thigh. However, when I assessed her, I was devastated to see numerous visible bruises. Courtney told me her mother had accidentally hit her with the belt buckle, not just the belt. I hugged Courtney, shed a few tears with her, and assured her that her mom loved her very much.

Calling Social Services was very emotional for me since I am on friendly terms with this family. I dreaded facing the parents, which as luck would have it, would be the following night at Courtney's 8th birthday party—a sleepover which Alexis was invited to attend. The morning of the party I received a call from Courtney's mother, who stated that Social Services had visited their house the previous evening, and Courtney had filled her mother in on the day's events. Mom was embarrassed, but wanted to make sure that I felt comfortable with Alexis spending the night at the sleepover, and to ask if I could come to the party a little early so we could talk.

When I arrived at their house, which is in an upscale neighborhood, mom welcomed me. Courtney's father did not seem very pleased to see me, and thankfully sat quietly in another room. Mom explained the events that led up to the belt incident and took full blame for everything. She said the social worker gave her some tips on disciplining her children a different way, and she was going to try to use them. She said she was grateful and would listen to any additional suggestions on discipline. Mom even thanked me for reassuring Courtney of her love.

The birthday party sleepover went very well. Alexis and Courtney are still best friends and love to spend time at each other's houses. Courtney recently confided in me that her mom has been much nicer and has stopped beating her with a belt. Although Courtney's mom still has very strict rules, she is working hard to find alternative ways to discipline her children.

Regrets

*The author's name has been omitted
to ensure that the identities of the individuals
in this story remain confidential.*

I am an elementary school nurse at heart. Toddlers are my favorite age group, I think because my sister had five kids and I spent a lot of time with them. I have spent most of my career in hospital pediatrics, ambulatory care, and then school nursing. Given a choice, I always chose elementary schools. So it was with some hesitation that I accepted a position at a high school when my husband retired and we moved back home. I had previously worked in high schools, but always as one of several schools that I covered—never one location full-time. But when you are suddenly the main breadwinner, you can't always be choosy about the jobs you accept.

During my first year at the high school, a sophomore girl named Maria would come in every day at lunchtime to take her medicine for cystic fibrosis. She was a pretty girl, very sweet, though tiny for her age. She was usually accompanied by one or two girlfriends. In the fall and spring, she would enter the local children's hospital for a "tune-up" as her doctor called it. While there, she would continue her studies through the hospital's educational staff.

My first regret is that I did not anticipate her engaging in risky behaviors, especially sexual activity. She seemed so innocent and child-like and never talked about boys. So it came as a shock to me in the spring of her junior year when she tearfully told me that she was pregnant. She was only a few weeks along at that time. We had a federal grant at our school that allowed us to work closely with students who were pregnant. While filling out the paperwork for the program, I asked her what she intended to do. She and I shared a religious belief that does not condone terminating pregnancies. However, due to her fragile health status, I suggested that perhaps her case would be an exception. She seemed undecided and I encouraged her to begin prenatal care, but also seek the advice of her pulmonologist about the wisdom of carrying this pregnancy to term. School dismissed for the summer. I thought about her often and could not envision a good outcome for this pregnancy.

When we returned to school in August, she came to tell me that she was still pregnant and intended to keep the baby. She still had a smile on her face and a positive attitude. Within a couple of weeks she was hospitalized. When I heard that she would remain in the hospital until she delivered, I went to visit her. She was having difficulty breathing, but tried to talk and was still smiling. Her mother was there and told me that she tried to convince her all summer to terminate the pregnancy, but her daughter refused. Maria really wanted this baby. Mom said the doctors were hoping to get her to 24 weeks before they took the baby. A few days later, when it was obvious that Maria would not make it, the doctors delivered the baby. Maria died shortly after the birth. The tiny baby lived four days and died also.

I regret that I did not anticipate this pregnancy. I regret that her doctors did not either. I regret that no one, not nurse, doctor, or parent, was able to convince her that not only her life, but also that of the baby's, were in jeopardy. I regret that she was not able to live to enjoy the baby that she so desperately wanted. I regret that the baby did not survive, either. And I regret that our faith played a major role in her decision.

But I do not regret knowing Maria. Sometimes there are no easy answers to difficult situations. She was a wonderful young girl with a beautiful smile and a great outlook on life. She would have made a wonderful mother.

While my heart is still with the younger children, I have settled into my job at the high school. These teenagers have their own set of problems as they struggle to become young adults. I hope that I am better able to anticipate some of their needs because of Maria.

Kids Have Adult Worries

By Vicki Senter, RN

A student ran into my office. He was short of breath, but managed to tell me that someone had fallen and was bleeding. He was unable to tell me what happened or who had fallen. I grabbed a first aid kit, locked my office, and went to the west hallway as directed by the student. My mind started racing through the standard protocol for any emergency. On the way, I overheard a page directing me to the library. My adrenaline started pumping a bit faster.

When I arrived, Brad was on the floor, and a puddle of blood was growing around his head. He was fully conscious, and attempting to stand.

"Brad, I need you to stay still for a minute. I need to check you out," I said.

He relaxed. I asked several teachers to clear the hallway for Brad's privacy. I put on some gloves and started my head to toe assessment. While doing this I was able to ask Brad what happened. He wasn't sure. He said he was walking with friends and then his head hit the door jamb of the fire doors. He denied feeling dizzy or anything odd before he hit the door. He thought he might have been accidentally shoved into the door. Finding no other trauma except the cut on his head, which had stopped bleeding, I let Brad slowly rise to a seated position. He reported he felt fine. I sent for the wheelchair. Brad was able to get into the wheelchair without incident. I brought him back to my office.

Once in the quiet calm of my office, one of the teachers told us that an ambulance was on the way. Brad became very upset. He began to yell, "I'm not going in no ambulance!" He tried to get out of the wheelchair to leave the nurse's office.

"Brad, stop. You need to calm down." I replied.

He shouted, "There is no way I am going in an ambulance!"

The teacher in the room said, "You have to, they're on their way!"

Brad started yelling again.

I asked the teacher if she could go to the main office to check if Brad's mom had been called. This gave me a moment alone with Brad. I crouched down so I could be at face level with him. I told him, "You don't have to go to the hospital by ambulance, but you do have to go to the hospital. You need stitches. Your bleeding has stopped so if Mom wants to bring you, she can. I can't stop the ambulance from coming. Once they get a call they have to come. They have to follow the laws that apply to them and that's one of them. They will check you out when they get here. You do not have to go with them."

Brad calmed down. Just then, the EMT's arrived. They checked him out. Brad's mom arrived while they were completing their assessment. They encouraged her to allow them to transport Brad by ambulance to the hospital. Before Brad's mom could reply, Brad started yelling that he wasn't going to the hospital by ambulance. His mom asked the EMT's if it would be okay if she brought him to the emergency room on her own. They discouraged the idea, but said it would be okay. They said it was imperative that she take him; he needed staples to close the wound. Mom assured them she would take him right away. They all left. I treated the next dozen or so students that entered my office, which left me little time to think about Brad.

About fifteen minutes before the final bell, Brad and his mom came back. They reported that Brad received eleven staples to close the wound on his head. They both thanked me for helping him. Brad left to go to his locker, giving me a chance to talk with his mother. She told me that they did not have insurance and that is why Brad was so upset at the possible ambulance ride. He was concerned about the cost. Brad gave his mom most of the money he earned from his part-time job. He was worried about his mom. Once I knew this, Brad's behavior made perfect sense.

That was the day I realized how different it is to be a teenager today. As a child, I never gave healthcare a second thought. My parents took care of it. Today is so different for our youth. They worry about so many things they can't control or change. Brad is living a teenager's life with adult worries and responsibilities. I take this lesson with me every day. Whenever a student enters my office, I remind myself that this young adult may have more worries than I know. It helps me to be more understanding, more compassionate.

They Took My Baby Away

*The author's name has been omitted
to ensure that the identities of the individuals
in this story remain confidential.*

When I received a phone call from one of Kelly's special education teachers one day in November, I had no idea I would soon be embroiled in the saddest, most frustrating situation I'd ever experienced as a school nurse. Nearly a quarter of the students at my high school are "special needs," with a grab bag of medically fragile and developmentally delayed conditions. These children are the reason I've remained at this high school for so long. They are sweet and gentle souls that give me an immense sense of purpose.

Kelly was a beautiful sixteen-year-old girl who suffered anoxia at birth, leaving her with cognitive abilities similar to that of a six-year-old. She was always happy and enthusiastic, and enjoyed participating in many of our Special Olympics sporting events. Her absolute favorite event was cheerleading. She often came to my office to show me her latest cheer routine, giggling as she tried to remember the choreography.

That day, her teacher told me she had overheard Kelly tell another student that she was pregnant. She was sent to me, and I gently asked her questions about why she thought she might be pregnant. It was like interviewing a small child, complete with magical thinking and rapid changes of subject. Kelly did confirm that she had not had a period, which she called her "girly thing," since school had started in August. Kelly also told me that she sometimes didn't have enough to eat and that "Mommy has problems paying our bills."

I consulted with our social worker, and we agreed that there was enough concern to contact Child Protective Services and file a report. Several days later Kelly's mother called me, extremely irate, to report "because of you CPS came to our house." She continued her tirade with accusations against the school, "If that girl is pregnant it happened at school. No one watches her there." I tried to assure her that we all just wanted to make sure Kelly was safe, and to determine if she was indeed pregnant. She finally agreed to make a doctor's appointment for her.

Kelly's "stepdad" showed up several days later with a receipt from the doctor, one of those barely legible, faint triplicate copies. He thrust it at me and proclaimed, "Here you go, we went to the doctor for a pregnancy test and it is negative. They also gave her a shot." I had no reason to doubt what he said. I assumed that she had indeed been tested, and had probably been given a Depo shot. I put the whole episode out of my mind, until we returned from Christmas break and her teacher once more contacted me: "Kelly is still saying she is pregnant."

The social worker and I waited in my treatment room for Kelly to come in, strategizing. At this point it had been nearly six months since Kelly last remembered having a period, and we decided to just be straightforward and ask to see her "tummy." She pulled up her hoodie and showed us her obviously swollen abdomen. Katie and I just looked at each other with grim determination to try to get this child some help.

What followed were several weeks of unbelievable frustration. When interviewed, Kelly insisted that the father of her baby was "probably my boyfriend. I'll wait to see if it looks like him." The only problem was that Kelly's boyfriend had moved out of state over a year ago, making it impossible for him to have fathered her baby. She just simply could not comprehend this, and it was obvious to us that she was acting evasive. Let's face it; six year olds have a way of telegraphing their lies. But she had dug in her heels and wasn't telling.

On top of everything else, she had received no prenatal care at this late stage of her pregnancy, and her mother kept failing to take her to scheduled medical appointments. Mom had a variety of excuses that she used, including her job, younger children, and the expense. As a former obstetrical nurse, I did as much as I could at school, checking her blood pressure, weight, and offering healthy snacks. But the reality was that we had no idea what her due date was. Once more, I had to file a report with CPS because of medical negligence.

Finally, Kelly was taken to the obstetrician in March (I hoped that the final CPS visit had forced her mother's hand), and we were at last given a due date: May 26th. She was 30 weeks pregnant, and I found it ironic that she had probably gotten pregnant during the first week of school and was due to deliver in our final week of school.

I still saw Kelly every day to check her blood pressure, offer her snacks, and to counsel this sweet girl. She was so child-like—one minute chattering excitedly about cheerleading and school events, and sometimes quiet and sad. One day when we were talking, I asked once again who she thought the father of her baby was. I don't know why this day was different than all the past days, but she finally decided to tell me the truth. She told me that it was her mother's live-in boyfriend, the man she called "my stepdad." In a little girl voice, she related what had happened, not making eye contact until she finished. At the end she looked up at me and asked, "Do you think they will take my baby away?"

What followed were weeks of dealing with caseworkers, documentation, police intervention, and worry. Once we knew her story, we hoped that she would immediately be taken out of the household and given a safe environment. She was made a ward of the state, but in reality she was still under the guardianship of her mother. A restraining order was placed on the mother's boyfriend, but many of us at school were sure that he was still allowed in the house. What would happen when the baby was delivered and there was positive proof that he had impregnated her?

We all worried constantly about Kelly's safety. I was forced to watch from the sidelines; Mom had forbidden Kelly from coming to me for her daily check-ups, as I had been the one to "turn them in." I still got updates through our social worker and her various special education teachers, but I no longer was able to keep a close eye on her or to offer her food and comfort. As her due date approached, I arranged for Kelly to always have someone accompany her to the restroom, and to watch her closely for signs of labor.

In the end, Kelly gave birth to a healthy baby boy during the final days of school. Over the summer break, I thought about her constantly and wondered what had happened. When we returned, Kelly sought me out during the first week of school, looking dejected.

"Nurse, they took my baby away. Can you tell them that I can have him back?"

It broke my heart, this child-like girl that had had her baby taken from her. I'm sure she felt as if she were being punished for something that was no fault of her own; but truly this family did not have the resources nor did Kelly have the mental capacity to care for a baby. I never heard what happened to the mother's boyfriend, but I have a hunch that he ran far away before the baby was born and evidence became available. For a while Kelly had weekly supervised visits with her baby, but they left her sad and depressed; eventually she just stopped going.

Kelly is still a student here, and she is now living with her new boyfriend and his family. He is a graduate of our special education program, and I hope she has found love and safety in their household. She seems happy, and we recently participated in a "Dancing with the Staff" program together. She loves cheerleading and dance, enjoys attending our sports events and school plays, and goes to special education programs after school. It has been three years since she gave birth, and she hardly ever mentions her baby anymore. She touched me deeply, this courageous woman-child, and I learned some valuable lessons from her. Although this experience was painful and frustrating, it helped me grow as a school nurse. I can only hope that Kelly's baby grows up healthy and happy, and that someday Kelly's emotional scars will heal.

Ready for Pizza

By Jenny Baggett, LPN

I began my career in school nursing twelve years ago at a middle school. One day, after being on the job for a couple of weeks, I was called upstairs to check on a student who had passed out in the hall. I was still very new and scared to death, so I ran upstairs and found a very skinny boy curled up on the floor. He was very weak and could not stand. I looked around and told the principal to call 9-1-1. One of his teachers was standing nearby and told me that he had an eating disorder. He was so skinny and weak that I was afraid he might die. The office had already called his mother and she arrived before the ambulance. She said that he was just acting up and told him to stand up and come home with her. She refused to let the ambulance take him to the hospital.

The following day, the student was back in school and came to the clinic. He stated that he had eaten breakfast but he still felt ill. I asked him if he felt like eating anything else. After talking with him at length, I called his mother and she informed me that he had been in a mental hospital for an eating disorder, and was acting as if he was getting sick again. She said she would take him to the doctor. However, several days passed and she never took him. He came to my office again complaining of not feeling well and stated, "I don't want to die." My heart broke. I thought *I have to do something NOW.* I called his mother and told her that she must take him to the doctor or I might find it necessary to call the Department of Children and Family Services.

The next morning I was notified that the boy had emergency surgery and was in the ICU. My supervisor and I visited the hospital and found he did not have an eating disorder; he had Crohn's Disease. His entire colon was blocked and, had he not had surgery, he could have died. When we walked into his room, I knew that he would be okay. He looked up at me with his big brown eyes, pointed to the tube in his nose, and said, "Get it out." I thought *He has some life back now.* I told him that when he got better I would treat him to pizza of his choice.

Two days later he was moved to a regular room and my husband and I visited him. When we entered the room he broke out with a big smile and said, "I'm hungry and I want pizza." He looked at my husband and asked, "Can he come too?"

"Would you like for him to join us?" I replied.

He said, "Yes, I think he can show me how it is done." My husband is a big man and I guess he thought my husband knew how to eat.

The student spent about 2-½ weeks in the hospital before returning to school. He came to the clinic and said he was ready for his pizza. I called my husband, who brought a pizza, and we ate together—a pizza party! Shortly after that the boy transferred out of my school; however, I still keep track of him. He has had multiple surgeries but is doing well.

I have been a nurse for 27 years, but have never felt as fulfilled as I did when I realized that I had a part in saving this boy's life. I love school nursing and plan on continuing my career as long as I can.

A Sad Student

By Kyra Manry, RN

A few years ago, I had a student, Jane, who was bipolar, schizophrenic, oppositional defiant disorder (ODD), obsessive-compulsive disorder (OCD), and depressed. She came into the health office often for many different complaints. She would have a headache, upset stomach, something that "hurt"— which made it difficult to gauge how much pain she was experiencing. As her visits became more frequent, she became more comfortable talking to me about herself. She would stop by for a "headache," talk to me for a few minutes, rest, and head back to class.

One day, she came in with a large purse, and started pulling out bottles of pills. She had four bottles in total. Jane quickly gave me two of the bottles, but kept the other two. She said she was feeling very, very depressed that day, and was thinking about taking all of the pills. I asked her why she felt she needed to take all of the pills. She replied that she was going to take them all because she knew if she did, the medicine would kill her. She had taken too many pills before, and said she was used to drinking activated charcoal.

I relied on the psychology training I received while in school, and applied my critical thinking skills as I continued to talk to her. I don't know why she felt compelled to give me the first two bottles, but I was glad she did. I was determined to get the other two before she left the clinic. I asked again why she wanted to take the pills. She was in tears, and kept telling me all of the reasons she should take them.

After almost two hours of talking, crying, and more talking, Jane gave me the other two bottles of pills. I had finally gotten her to change her mind. I kept her in the clinic until her parents arrived. Our school counselor had been off campus, so I was relieved that this student felt comfortable enough to come to me with her problem. Because of that, I always make an effort to talk with my students, and make sure they know the health office is a safe place to visit. I know I saved Jane's life that day. She ended up dropping out of school, and later took courses to earn her GED. A few years later, she stopped into my office to thank me for helping her through her "tough time."

Acting Upon a Nursing Instinct

By Rayleen J. Bradley, RN, IBCLC

Routine lice screening is a major part of my school nurse duties, and also gives me a great opportunity to see my students on a regular basis. As each of them steps up for their hair to be examined, I observe skin conditions, evaluate hygiene, notice stitches or bruising, and have a bit of conversation.

As I greeted each 4th grade student prior to the "toothpick exam," my eyes were drawn to a particular young lady. Her flat affect, pallor skin tone, and listlessness aroused concern about her medical well-being. I took my time looking through her hair and struck up a conversation. It was mostly one-sided, due to her lack of participation. I finished the exam and watched her somberly return to her seat.

Upon returning to the main office, I sat down with the staff that has known this class of students since kindergarten. I asked if this particular girl had any current medical conditions, or was being treated for an illness that I was unaware of. There was nothing in her record.

My nursing instinct kicked in, and I decided to call the student's parents. I asked if anything seemed different about their daughter. The father answered almost immediately with a sense of relief.

"We noticed that she grows tired quickly, and has lost her appetite," he stated.

We talked some more, and he continued to explain, "She also has lost interest in activities she normally enjoys." I described what I saw in the health room during lice screening. The father then said, "She is not her same old self. We thought about calling her doctor, but haven't gotten around to it yet— I'm going to call their office today!"

I received a phone call from her parents within a few days with results of the doctor's exam. Test results revealed a severely low thyroid function. The doctor began treatment immediately. The parents were extremely grateful for my call, as it gave them an objective point of view that confirmed their observations.

As I was preparing to start instruction for the 4th grade girls' health class in the spring of that school year, I spotted the young girl at her desk. What an amazing transformation I saw before me! Her skin had a beautiful pink glow; she had a beaming smile and a happy demeanor! She came up to me after class and told me how great she was now feeling.

That is why I became a school nurse...for moments like that!

Tiny Megan

The author's name has been omitted
to ensure that the identities of the individuals
in this story remain confidential.

Megan was a pretty little girl, the smallest in her class. At home, she was the youngest of five and sometimes got lost in the shuffle. Megan was born with Phenylketonuria (PKU). Her body would not break down phenylalanine. Like all children with PKU, she was not supposed to consume meat, milk, or regular breads. She should have been on special formula since birth with a very restricted diet.

Megan's home environment was a little chaotic. Her recently divorced mother was working nights and doing her best to care for the children. She was not able to send food to school, and in the mornings when her siblings served breakfast, they gave Megan whatever she wanted: bacon, eggs, and chocolate milk. Mom also missed many of the planning sessions the school staff held to facilitate Megan's health and learning. In addition, English was not the family's first language, so you can imagine how hesitant her mother was to initiate contact with professionals.

In the beginning, her classroom teachers brought juice and foods for classroom snacks. I tried to convince Megan's mother that although she didn't feel sick when she ate foods with phenylalanine, it would hurt her brain because they were toxic to her. I contacted the hospital where she was receiving care, and they said that her mother didn't seem to need a translator and was always in agreement with the plan. In my mind, this was just not working.

The school staff and I first started to get involved by requesting a translator be present for all medical appointments. We then asked for a waiver to have Megan's formula sent to the school, and began a daily schedule. Megan was allowed to mix her formula in the classroom at 10:00 a.m. and 2:00 p.m., and we brought her the formula to take at lunch. We also began giving her a daily medicine, Kuvan, which she should have been taking to help break down phenylalanine. She wasn't getting the Kuvan at home on a regular basis. We would administer it five days a week at lunch and send home the correct dose in envelopes for the weekend.

Initially, Megan was very shy and wary of our monitoring her food tray at breakfast and lunch (and controlling what she had for classroom parties). But as she began to understand that we were not punishing her, she became more animated. Since our health center is lucky enough to have student nurses, each semester a student would be assigned to have lunch with her and talk about any concerns. We were also able to get noodles and special flour from the hospital and, using our PKU cookbooks, the nursing students began cooking "treats" to supplement fruits and vegetables from the school lunch. Those wonderful students were even able to make pizza for her for classroom parties. Slowly we got her on track.

We can't cure Megan's genetic anomaly, but we have been able to help her stay on a better diet, begin to trust healthcare providers, and let her know she is safe and loved at school.

What the Dental Program Has Done for the Kids of Galena

By Amy Price, RN

Imagine waking up during the night with a toothache. After tossing and turning, you are finally able to go back to sleep. The next morning you are hungry for some breakfast, but it hurts too much to eat. You proceed to school and are expected to listen, participate in activities, and learn all kinds of new information. But it just isn't that simple. You see, you haven't slept well in several weeks, so you find yourself dozing. You haven't eaten anything solid for several days, so your belly is rumbling and causing you to feel nauseous as the bile keeps coming up in your throat. Your mouth is throbbing and all you can think about is how to get relief from the excruciating pain. The teacher finally sends you to the nurse to see if you are sick.

Upon examination, the nurse finds that several molars have deep cavities in them. The nurse calls your mother, gives you ibuprofen, and applies orasol gel. It doesn't help; the damage is too severe. Mom doesn't have any way to pay for dental care, and even if she did there wouldn't be any transportation. The cycle continues and eventually the pain subsides.

Unfortunately, this scenario has played out multiple times with the students here in Galena. All of that changed during the fall of 2007. The Community Health Center of Southeast

Kansas Dental Clinic approached us about starting a dental program at the school. The need was so great we jumped at the chance.

First, it consisted of simple screenings with an occasional trip to the dental clinic in Pittsburg for those students that were in pain. Second, the cleanings started. We had approximately 90 students the first year. We took a bus to the clinic on a couple of occasions for students to have dental work done. Finally, our current program began in 2009. The students come to the school clinic for teeth cleanings, x-rays, fluoride treatments, fillings, and even extractions. On occasion we have to take a trip to the clinic for root canals.

You may be skeptical and think that it doesn't work, but our numbers have increased from 90 kids in 2008, to 135 kids in 2009, and in 2010 we provided care to 345 children. Good news travels fast. Our kids love coming to the clinic. They love going back to class and showing their teachers their shiny teeth. Two students have had composite bridges. Before they were self-conscious about their smiles, covering their mouths when they spoke or smiling with closed lips. Now they smile with pride. We no longer have kids missing multiple days of school or lunch trays that haven't been touched because of pain. Usually a simple phone call offering the clinic's services and a consent form sent home are all that is needed for the child to be seen the next day. The kids and parents know that we are here to help.

It is time for somebody to step up and help those kids that cannot help themselves. It is time for someone to reach out to them and let them know that they are cared about. How can we expect them to learn and thrive when their basic needs are not met? It was time for us as a school district to be proactive and meet their physical needs.

II.

Beyond the Job Description

"To me, being a school nurse is more than just the school day. Rather, being a school nurse encompasses all aspects of my students' lives. Even on a Saturday morning when I am tired."

–Patricia VanHavermaat, BSN, RN, NCSN

Forever Changed

By Tina Clark, RN, BSN

Starting kindergarten is supposed to be a happy and exciting time for both parents and students.

No one was expecting a diagnosis of leukemia on the third day of school. As a school nurse for six years at the time, I needed to do a review of leukemia. I was scared for this little girl, Sarah, and her family. I was afraid I would not be able to provide the care needed for her while at school.

Sarah missed much of her first semester of kindergarten due to treatments. When she was in school, I worried about those childhood illnesses like chicken pox, stomach viruses, the flu and such. Additionally, Sarah's dad, Jeff, is a big bear-like man, who teaches high school in the city. At first I feared Jeff just as much as leukemia. He was scared and angry, not knowing what the outcome would be for his daughter.

Sarah made it through the first year. She was back at school and doing well in first grade. Treatments were less interruptive because the lab came to the school. Sarah was becoming a hard stick. Most kids her age would have their favorite stuffed friend, but I was becoming Sarah's stick friend. We would laugh and cry together through all the treatments.

Sarah, a class friend, and I would do crafts or go to movies after school together, giving mom and dad a break from a routine they did not choose. Sarah and I became close, through losing her hair three times, days of nausea, and more vomiting. My office was a friendly and non-judgmental place.

I found the other side of Jeff, the softer side, and we became friends. Last year was Sarah's final year as one of my students; she was moving on to middle school. I knew I was going to miss her, but I did not realize how much. On the last day of school, I was doing pretty well until Jeff gave me a huge bear hug and we cried all day together. He asked if I could transfer to the middle school.

The relationship created by leukemia has changed me. I am more confident and understanding of what families may be going through outside the home. I learned anger is not always what it seems. I am a big believer that school nursing is more about relationships with students and families than diagnosis and strong clinical skills.

I Almost Didn't Go

By Patricia VanHavermaat, BSN, RN, NCSN

It was a big family, with six kids being raised by their grandmother and sickly grandfather. The parents came and went, but were so dependent on drugs that responsibility was the last thing on their minds.

The kids ranged in age from eight to fourteen. I had been the school nurse for each of them at one time or another. Their grandmother was rough around the edges, resilient, and did the very best she could with the resources she had. Their grandfather was in renal failure and went to dialysis three times a week. He was wheelchair bound. Both loved their grandchildren, but the challenge of caring for them was, more often than not, overwhelming.

Over the years I made many home visits for numerous reasons: to inform them about individual health plans, to teach how to get rid of lice, to drop off Thanksgiving and Christmas food baskets, or helping with whatever was needed.

The kids were often a challenge for me as their school nurse. I often had to explain why certain clothes were not appropriate for school and life in general. I frequently needed to re-teach hygiene. I repeatedly discussed the health risk of drug use and inappropriate sexual behavior. Their physical, environmental, and psychosocial needs were great.

One day I read in the local Wednesday newspaper that their grandfather had passed away. The rosary was planned at 9:00 a.m. that Saturday followed by a funeral mass. I decided

I needed to go to support my students as well as to show them I really cared about them. Saturday morning when I woke up, I was still very tired and thought *I just won't go.* But I felt an even stronger sense that I should.

I pulled into the church parking lot, and saw about fifteen or twenty people standing at the top of the steps at the entrance of the church. When I climbed the steps, all of a sudden one of my students yelled, "It's Nurse Trish!" She and her siblings ran to meet and greet me, as did their grandmother. It was then that the grandmother introduced me to the rest of the family— *all* of the people on the steps!

After a quick greeting, I went inside the church to await the rosary. I was surprised that no one else was in the church. After all was said and done, I was the only non-family member at the rosary, and one of five non-family members at the funeral service.

And to think...I almost didn't go. To me, being a school nurse is more than just limited to the school day. Rather, being a school nurse encompasses all aspects of my students' lives. Even on a Saturday morning when I am tired.

A Happy Ending

*The author's name has been omitted
to ensure that the identities of the individuals
in this story remain confidential.*

For some women, that long-awaited pink positive sign is a reason for celebration: a baby! For 17-year-old Lucy that same sign was definitely NOT a reason to celebrate.

Lucy, a high school senior, came to me one Friday morning in great distress over an unplanned pregnancy. This young lady was an excellent student from a solid two-parent home. She had already been accepted into college to pursue a degree in education. She informed me she had only had relations once. She had taken a home pregnancy test three times and was certain she was pregnant. She cried in my office about how upset her mom would be and said, "My dad will kill me." She assured me she still planned to go to college and become a teacher, and planned to keep and raise her baby. At that time, the father had no interest in being involved in the baby's life.

I work in a small town where I myself went to high school. Because of this, I personally know many of my students' parents. This was a set of parents I knew well. I knew her mother would be heartbroken, and that her father would initially be quite upset. I visited with Lucy regarding her parents' reactions, and shared with her a parent's perspective. We discussed how she could still build a future even though it would be more difficult and challenging than originally planned. I suggested she write down her thoughts and the points she wanted to get across to her parents before she talked with them. I offered to be with her when she initially spoke with her parents; however, she turned me down. She opted to write a long letter to her parents that she could read aloud so she would not forget to say anything she wished to mention.

All weekend I thought about Lucy. I hoped things were going well at home between her and her parents. First thing Monday morning, Lucy came to see me. The full report was that, yes, her mother had cried and, yes, her father had yelled, but over the weekend they all came together and were making plans for Lucy to graduate high school and still attend college while being a new mom. Her parents helped her over the next few years and were great supporters and mentors for both their daughter and their new grandson. The father of the baby continued to remain out of the picture.

Last summer I received a college graduation announcement and an invitation to a celebration for Lucy. I was so proud of her. Her road was harder than normal but in 4-½ years she had accomplished her goal. This young mother is now a teacher and her little guy is a happy, well-adjusted kindergartner.

I am Disappointed

*The author's name has been omitted
to ensure that the identities of the individuals
in this story remain confidential.*

Not so long ago, as a high school nurse, I was presented with a student that had an emergency bandsaw accident in woodshop class. The student presented a very calm, very stoic attitude. He was amazing, considering he lost most of his fingers on one hand.

Over the course of his recovery and after, the student, his father, and I developed a friendly, working relationship. I was very surprised when almost five years later they decided to sue the school district, the high school principal, and the shop teacher. I have since been subpoenaed as a witness for the school district, as I was the nurse who took care of this student until he was transported to the hospital. The school district's lawyers instructed me that I should no longer talk to my student or his father.

When this young man graduated, I really wanted to visit his home, give him a gift card, and share my pride in his accomplishment. I called the district lawyers and was strongly advised not to do this, as this simple little act could be construed in court as an attempt at a bribe. The attorney and I discussed this at length. I even suggested just sending a card and not visiting in person, but was told this too was not advisable. If I did, I would do so at my own risk and my actions could be construed as a detriment to the school district, regardless of the fact that I wasn't named in the suit.

After agonizing and praying over the decision, I decided not to see the student or send congratulations in the form of a gift card. I am disappointed that my student and his father brought a lawsuit against the school district. I am disappointed that as a consequence, I had to do what the school attorney thought was prudent. I am disappointed. I look to the day when this school nurse can acknowledge her student's educational success and physical recovery. Until then, I am disappointed that an accident can hold friendships in limbo.

A Fitful Fifth Grader

By Sam Bastian, RN, MS, APNP-BC

A fifth grader came into my office, out of control and seething. She said she got her first period that morning and she didn't like it.

"I AM NEVER GOING TO HAVE IT AGAIN!" she yelled.

Her eyes were red from crying, her face was all puffy, and her hair was all messed up. I tried to explain that I could see she was upset, and that many girls became distressed when they got their first period. I gave her supplies for the day. She stomped out of my office.

An hour later as I was walking through the gym, I saw her sitting on the floor, literally pulling her hair out. Another girl ran over to her and said, "Hey, Mary, come and be on our team." She looked up at her with a hormonally-induced rage and said, "Sure, NOW you want to be my friend—no way!"

I had never seen a more tortured soul. I stopped, scooped her up and said, "C'mon, you are coming with me." I told the gym teacher that the girl needed to come with me as we left the gym. I was headed to another building to work with some senior citizens and instructed her to follow me.

"I don't want to talk to you!" she said.

"No need to talk, just stick with me; it's not about you," I replied.

She quietly followed as I made my rounds with the seniors, and accepted the tissues I offered for her drippy nose. The crying eventually stopped, and she was able to get control of herself. Later that morning, I returned her to class.

On my way out of the building that night, her teacher stopped me and said, "I feel so bad about Mary."

"She will be okay; she was just surprised and overwhelmed," I said.

The teacher said, "No, I feel bad because it is my fault she got her period. She has been premenstrual for so long that every night I have prayed *Please God just let her get her period!* But now she is even worse!" I assured the teacher she really didn't have that much power and we would all weather this storm.

That was five years ago. Mary grew up, graduated from our school, and now comes back to volunteer with the little ones during the summer. She is a beautiful high school student and although I haven't asked her, I'm sure she has had a few more periods.

The Truth About Real School Nursing

By Caroline Champion, RN, MSN, ICSN

In the years that I have been part of the nursing profession, I have been privy to numerous negative opinions expressed about the specialty of school nursing. I remember first hearing comments while I was attending college. Several of my instructors implied that school nursing was not "real nursing," that none of the students should consider it because it took no special skills and would not "challenge the intellect." Later I heard that others viewed the role as a transition between their career in "real" nursing and retirement.

Many hold the dubious assumption that school nursing is an undemanding assignment and, therefore, will allow them an abundance of free time and leisure before their departure from the workforce. Even though most registered nurses have never practiced outside the hospital setting, some assume that they have the qualifications to step into the position and work within and about the educational system. How often have I heard, "Oh, a school nurse? Well that must be a nice little job with summers off." Other nurses would not even consider the position because it is not "bona fide" nursing. Every one of these nurses has the mistaken notion that all a certified school nurse does is sit in her office and perform first aid. Nothing could be further from the truth.

School nursing is a specialty similar to emergency room, hospice, and ICU nursing—but in many ways, even more specific. The requirements for this position are multifaceted. In order to apply for admission, one must hold a license as a registered nurse for at least two years, complete a bachelor's degree in nursing, pass three educational foundation classes, attend 30 lecture hours in an accredited certified school nurse program, and perform a clinical rotation with a certified school nurse. Passing a basic skills test, a specialty exam in school nursing, and becoming certified in vision and hearing screening are also part of the process. Only then may one apply for certification in school nursing.

In addition to the educational requirements that are mandated, a successful certified school nurse must possess special skills. As in the other areas of nursing expertise, not everyone is suited for the particular demands that are placed on the specialty of school nursing.

The job requires one to be accomplished with dexterity, proficiency, and cleverness. One must be able to perform independently and autonomously. As the only health professional in the school, the nurse must discharge her duties with authority. There are no other nurses with which to confer, nor is there a physician on call to take over in an emergency. The nurse must also know how the educational system works and how nursing is integrated into it. Pediatric nursing skills must be sharp and the nurse should have a working knowledge of state requirements and immunizations. One has to be able to organize, prioritize, and plan programs and initiate policies. The nurse needs to be an active case manager and work together with a multitude of disciplines— such as administrators, psychologists, teachers, and parents— to do the best for the children that they serve.

One should be assertive, but also know when diplomacy should be utilized. Good communication skills are essential in order to work effectively with administration and parents. Teaching skills must be honed and the nurse should be able to perform many different tasks during the course of the day. One needs to be flexible and adapt with regards to triaging events, demands, and situations as needed. Something that has been planned may have to be rearranged due to a crisis situation or because another priority has occurred.

A school nurse must be good at everything, not only emergency care, but also nursing assessment, chronic illness management, complex medical conditions, epidemiology, prevention, safety, teaching, screening, communicating, care management, policy development, grant-writing, employee health, community health, legal issues, politics, advocacy, care plan development, pharmacology, computer documentation, and now RTI, Response to Intervention.

The school nurse may also be the attention deficit resource person. Part of that role includes case finding and screening, coordination of services with other disciplines, performing comprehensive assessments, providing liaison services, advocating for and educating the child and family, and monitoring and evaluating student and program outcomes.

The capable school nurse should be skilled at producing newsletters, bulletin board materials, staff in-services, and school board presentations. While the nurse is doing all this, they must be able to speak the language of education. Even though the nurse sees his or her role as providing health care, educators will see the nurse as a supporter of the real job of schools—educating children.

Within the school system, one is more than a nurse. The nurse is a bridge between the healthcare community and the school. As the quote says, "One cannot educate a child who is not healthy and one cannot keep a child healthy who is not educated."

School nurses must strive for best practice, adhering to their state's nurse practice act while also working in a non-medical, unpredictable setting. Societal changes have influenced schools tremendously, and children today come to school with more needs and health issues than they did in the past. Certified school nursing is much more than putting on bandages.

A Precious Life

By Kyra Manry, RN

I recall the day an 18-year-old epileptic student in her first trimester of pregnancy was carried into the clinic. She had just had an epileptic seizure and our truancy officer, along with a male student, brought her to the clinic and laid her on the bed.

I am fortunate to be on campus every day with my students, so I was familiar with her medical condition. When she was brought in, she was choking on her own saliva and having trouble breathing. I rolled her on her side and put her head just off the side of the bed. I began back percussion to try and clear the airway of the large amount of mucus; I did not have any way to suction her, which I knew she desperately needed. I had to think quickly and work with what I had.

As I stood next to the bed, even with her shoulders, the truancy officer supported her legs. She started to gasp for air. I hoped the gasps meant she was about to recover, as she spat up mucus over several minutes.

Suddenly, she stopped breathing. I yelled at the truancy officer to call 9-1-1, and I pulled her back on the bed. I grabbed my emergency kit, pulled out the resuscitator bag, and began rescue breathing for her until the paramedics arrived. They transported her to a nearby hospital for treatment where she and the baby survived.

On November 29, 2009, she had a C-section and delivered a beautiful baby girl.

The War

By Patricia VanHavermaat, BSN, RN, NCSN

As I stood looking into the casket, life passed through the recesses of my memory. I was her school nurse in 3rd through 8th grades. She was a child of innocence with a zest for learning and life. Her bright sparkling eyes and infectious giggles were contagious. Her visits to the nurse's office could turn a mundane day into a breath of fresh air! The vast majority of her trips to the school nurse were just to check in and get a dose of TLC, and yes, the occasional bandage or peppermint for the tummy.

The end of 6th grade left her excited and a bit "scared" about leaving the elementary years behind and heading into middle school. This became an almost daily topic of discussion the last few weeks of her 6th grade visits. I was very glad I could assure her that I would be her middle school nurse too.

Her 7th grade school year started fairly predictable: bright shining eyes, butterflies playing ping-pong in the stomach, and a flushed excitement! She met new classmates from the other elementary schools that feed into the middle school. She had some good experiences and some not so good. Developmentally, she was indeed finding herself and making choices that could affect the rest of her life. Gradually, her only trips to the nurse occurred when she was sent by the principal because of an injury received while fighting.

Whenever I did see her in my office or on campus, it was disheartening to see that her zest was gone. The light in her eyes was fading, and eventually faded altogether into a blank stare. Any attempt, and there were many, to engage my student resulted in failure. She was always, *always* respectful, yet she also had built an impenetrable wall around her. I referred her to the school counselor, I talked to her parents and grandparents, and I attended SAT (Student Assistant Team) meetings to give input and share concern. Covertly, and not so covertly, I assessed her for gang involvement, substance use, and any other troublesome behavior. I gave subtle, and not so subtle, substance abuse educational moments along with the school-wide anti-drug assemblies.

As I watched her grow during the 7th and 8th grade years, I was sickened and alarmed to see her slipping away. What's worse, I did not seem to be able to fix it. Whenever she and I did have contact, I made sure she knew I cared and that I was available. She began 9th grade at the high school but did not finish the year, nor did she finish high school. She was a cashier at a local store and on occasion would ring up my purchases. Any attempt at conversation was tense, strained, and mostly one-sided. I remember the last time I saw her. While she scanned my items, I actually saw a faint smile, which gave me a slight glimmer of hope.

As I viewed this precious, precious child in her casket, the parts of her life that I shared with her passed by in memory. The anguish, the angst, and the sorrow I felt were immeasurable. Here lay an eighteen-year-old child with an eight-month-old baby waiting to be born in her womb, both dead. "Friends" had intravenously injected a mixture of several illegal drugs directly into a vein in her arm; she and her unborn child died of "an accidental overdose."

Walking into the reception area of the funeral home that evening, I had been greeted by excited shouts of, "It's Nurse Trish!" and was fiercely hugged. As I shook hands and greeted my former students, it was not lost on me that the vast majority were under the influence. And it was not lost on them that I knew, and that I did not condone their bad choices. As I passed into the family room to give my deepest condolences to parents, siblings, and grandparents, I was stricken by the realization that those in this group were under the influence as well. I paid my last respects at the open casket with the gut wrenching realization that my student died under the influence of drugs; drugs that were still a major part of some of her family's and friends' lives.

As I drove home my mind reeled! *What happened? Where, when, and how did things go so wrong? What could have been done? What can be done? What a tragic loss!* And, truth be told, I also remember thinking that she is not hurting anymore and her baby will not be born into a life of drugs. And of course as her school nurse for so many years, I thought *Could I have helped prevent this tragedy?*

We have just finished a week in memory and in honor of DEA Agent Enrique "Kiki" Camarena, who in 1985 gave the ultimate sacrifice in the war on drugs: his life, just as my student and her unborn child lost their lives. One was working so hard to stop the insidious drug trafficking and one was working so hard to stop the pain of her life. Red ribbons flapping in the breeze, goggles that "make you walk and react" as if drunk, a demonstration from a drug sniffing dog, anti-drug slogans on lip balm and frisbees, and red ribbons on lapels; none of it really makes a difference. It is easy to say, "Well if we influence just one kid, then it is good," and while it may be good for that one kid, what about the many, many others?

The war is in our own backyard. We are the front line. How many more students will be lost?

A Wish Come True

By Evelyn Max, RN

I never knew how much one student could change my life forever. It was during my second year working as a middle school nurse that I met Diamond, a sixth grade student who had been diagnosed with bone cancer the previous year. Although Diamond could use crutches, most of the time he used a wheelchair to make his way through the crowded hallways in school.

In early January, when all the gym classes were playing basketball, Diamond made a comment to one of the gym teachers that he would love to participate in the game—and not just as the scorekeeper. The teacher, touched by Diamond's yearning to be able to do something that he loved, came to me to see if I knew of a way to get Diamond a sports wheelchair. Knowing how important this was to Diamond, I immediately started investigating.

Using the internet as my tool, I contacted several manufacturers of sports wheelchairs. After days of searching one of the companies replied to my inquiry, and asked me to write a letter explaining why it was so important for Diamond to have this special wheelchair. Although writing is something that I generally try to avoid as much as possible, I quickly went to work on this most important request.

In my letter, I explained that despite his terminal illness, Diamond was determined to participate and be a part of the physical education class as much as possible; however, his existing wheelchair was not capable of sports-like movement. Knowing his parents would not be able to purchase a specialized wheelchair on their own, I continued to explain his family's financial situation. As Diamond's medical bills increased, his family was struggling to provide for their daily needs. A new wheelchair was just not possible. I asked the sports wheelchair company if they would be willing to donate or lend one to Diamond so that he would have the ability to join in the physical education classes and have fun with his friends.

About a week later, to everyone's surprise, a huge box was delivered to the school. Inside was a brand new, state-of-the-art, sports wheelchair! We quickly assembled the chair, and requested that Diamond be pulled out of class and sent to the nurse's office. As soon as he rounded the corner into the health office, I vividly remember how his face lit up at the sight of the new wheelchair! He tested it out immediately. He was finally able to play basketball with his friends, and not just be a spectator from the sidelines. This new-found enthusiasm that could only have happened with the blessing of this new wheelchair inspired his friends, other students, and all the teachers that knew of Diamond's situation.

In May of that same year, the school held a student-faculty basketball game in honor of Diamond. The game was also a fundraiser to aid in his family's mounting medical bills. Even though Diamond was in a great amount of pain that night, one would never have known by just looking at his smiling face. With the aid of his new sports wheelchair, he was able to shoot some hoops with the other students before the basketball game. The evening was truly a special occasion, as the entire school gathered to honor Diamond and support his family.

Unfortunately, the night of the fundraiser basketball game was the last day that most of the students and staff saw Diamond and his smiling face. He was unable to return to school because his illness had advanced. Diamond passed away a few weeks after that memorable evening, but as a community we never forgot how happy he was in the last few months of his life. This would never have been possible without the generous company's gift of the sports wheelchair.

I still think about Diamond every day, and how he changed my life. I am sure that everyone he came in contact with feels the same way. After Diamond's passing, the school built a garden to honor his memory. As you enter the building, a beautifully mounted basketball jersey with Diamond's name and number hangs in the hallway. Along with this visible recognition of such an inspirational young boy who lived life to the fullest, a plaque hangs above it that reads:

In loving memory of Diamond
He loved basketball
He loved his family and friends
But most of all, he loved life

III.

Finding Inspiration

∞

"In nursing, anything can happen…"
–Maria Tela, RN

A Privilege to Know Him

By Kathryn D. VanGelder, RN, BSN

I first met Kelvin during the fall of 2007. He was a large, beautiful, boisterous, teddy bear of a boy that never failed to make me smile. While he preferred the social aspect of high school life, he did occasionally participate in class work. Many teachers worked very hard to get Kelvin to complete his assignments, but he would only do the assignments that sparked his interest. Kelvin spent many hours in the "back hall" awaiting discipline from the vice principal for his latest infraction.

During the summer of 2009, Kelvin was involved in a car accident and, as a result, was in a coma for two months. He was diagnosed with a brain injury. The doctors seemed certain he would not leave the hospital alive, and if he did, his cognitive abilities would be greatly diminished. The odds were in his favor, as he returned to school in September with a tracheostomy and a wheelchair (the latter of which I never saw him use). The brain injury caused a right-sided weakness, and he used a cane on his bad days.

When he first returned to school, he spent the majority of his school day in the health room. I would perform tracheostomy care and tried my best to educate him on how to care for himself so that he could be more independent. He was unable to speak, but was very patient with me as I learned to lip-read. Sometimes I would just throw my hands up in the air and make him write down what he wanted to tell me, and he did so with a smile.

As you might expect, he was falling behind in his schoolwork, and I would have to guide him out of the health room and onto the elevator for his next class. Funny thing is, he was the very same Kelvin as before his accident, aside from his physical limitations. His ability to understand was there, but his ambition to succeed in class was not. As time passed, he grew more independent and would make an effort to go to class, coming to the health room for tracheostomy care and to eat lunch with me. He even got to the point where he could whisper. He would call me "Ma," which always made me smile.

Sadly, Kelvin died on Valentine's Day of 2010 from probable pneumonia. At his visitation, there were tears, but there was also laughter as we remembered his very special personality and all of his antics. Kelvin touched the lives of the students and the faculty at the high school and he will forever be in our hearts.

Every day, I try to see my students with the same eyes I saw Kelvin. He has made me a more patient nurse, helping me to realize that each student has bruises, whether they are visible or not. I remember that it is always important to show love and kindness, because you never know when that special soul will be taken from you.

Remember, I Love You

By Patricia VanHavermaat, BSN, RN, NCSN

After years of nursing in hospitals, my husband and my mother prayed me out of a sixty mile round trip commute and into school nursing in the same school district from which I graduated. I wasn't nearly as pleased as they were when I interviewed and was hired. Nevertheless, I quickly adapted and loved my job as a school nurse. About five-and-a-half months into that first year, my mother suddenly died. It was a blow that was unexpected and swift. My heart ached.

I was off work for a week on bereavement leave. When I returned, it was good to see the kids and school staff. However, I just could not seem to work through my grief. One day I was browsing through sale books and came across a title, *Remember, I Love You.* I was compelled to buy it and started reading almost immediately. It was a very touching true story written about the death of the author's wife and their years of marriage before her death. The author was raised in a non-demonstrative family. He knew he was loved, it just wasn't said nor were hugs given. His wife, on the other hand, was from a family where hugs and "I love you" abounded.

Once after an argument the husband felt that surely his wife no longer loved him. He moped about until finally, in exasperation, she said, "Charles, don't you know that even when I'm mad at you and don't particularly like you at the moment, that I love you? Remember, I love you!" The author goes on to share the black hole of grief he felt after the death of his wife. His description was what I was feeling over the loss of my mother.

This story stayed on my mind and in my heart as I continued my job as a school nurse. So much so that one day after witnessing yet another shaming of a student by an angry adult, I decided I needed to let kids know how special and important they were. I began to tell them "Remember, I love you." For a week when each student was leaving the nurse's office, I would say, "Remember, I love you." The kids would giggle and run out or just leave. After a week I decided this was not the answer to letting my students know they were special and important because they just didn't seem to respond.

On the following Monday I no longer told the kids I loved them. Some of my students said, "Nurse Trish, don't you love me anymore?" or "I love you Nurse Trish," or simply reached up around my waist and gave me a hug. At the end of the school day, all but two of my students had said or had done something to make me realize that letting them know they were loved really had made a difference. Of course, I immediately began letting them know once again that I loved them—elementary, middle school, high school, at all levels.

It is important to note that I didn't just say the words, I truly meant them and my students seemed to know this. If there happened to be a student I just couldn't say it to, I still showed affection with smiles and a "that a boy/girl," or some other sincere affirmation. It might also be important to note that not only did my mother and husband pray me into school nursing; God blessed me in a very special way.

The blessing God gave me? Seventeen years of kids that I truly loved. Letting them know I loved them was important to them and to me. They each were a gift from God. It is hard to grieve when showered with so much love.

The Rewarding Duties of a School Nurse

By Darlene Fields, LPN

Being a school nurse at Appalachia Elementary School requires the ability to multi-task. Seeing forty to fifty kids a day is nothing compared to what some schools see, but here at AES it's the peaceful feeling of knowing that you can make a child smile with only a hug or a word of praise. I love my job. Sure I may not always enjoy the paperwork that comes with being a school nurse. Or the headaches I get from calling not-so-understanding parents regarding their children's medical needs. And not many parents appreciate when you call home to explain how to eradicate head lice. I don't like picking the pesky little critters out myself, especially when I end up scratching my own head until I make it sore. But the pros far outweigh the cons.

Now here is why I love my job:

- It's the fulfillment you get when you pick the crayon out of little Tommy's nose, and he looks up at you and says, "Thank you, Nurse Darlene."
- The comfort you give a child when his nose is bleeding, and the next day he comes in with his snack pack pudding cup and stretches it out in his little hand, thanking you for saving his life.

It's being able to calm a mother down when she is shaking and scared because her daughter fell and has an egg-sized knot on her head.

It's being there to administer a breathing treatment or inhaler when a dreaded asthma attack occurs.

It's both fun and exhausting when I disrupt the Pre-K class by hopping down the hallway and having the children join in, laughing all the way. Especially while their teacher tries to pretend she's not angry with me for encouraging them to make noise, after she spent months teaching them to be quiet and walk in a straight line.

The joy of watching a child's face light up because you give them a piece of candy or a sticker, and they act like they've never had candy before.

It's fire running through your veins when Sarah falls off the monkey bars, sprains an ankle, and you're praying the pain will go away.

Running down the hallway to get to a room because Brandy is having a seizure and the teacher is about to faint.

The love you feel when you get paper cards made from all the kindergarten and first grade children thanking you on Nurse's Day.

The kind words of encouragement you receive from the teachers and administration for all the hard work you do.

It's knowing Amanda can see the board after you discovered she needed glasses by performing a day of vision and hearing screening.

The satisfaction of Joe having tubes surgically placed in his ears because you referred him to an audiologist.

The adrenaline rush you get when you're riding in an ambulance to transport a teacher who has had a heart attack.

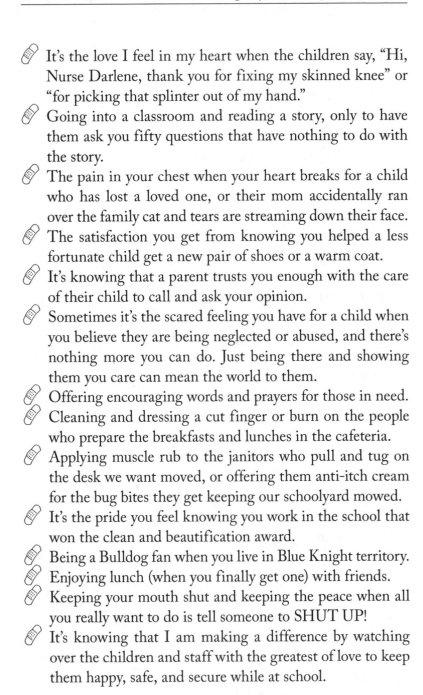

It's the love I feel in my heart when the children say, "Hi, Nurse Darlene, thank you for fixing my skinned knee" or "for picking that splinter out of my hand."

Going into a classroom and reading a story, only to have them ask you fifty questions that have nothing to do with the story.

The pain in your chest when your heart breaks for a child who has lost a loved one, or their mom accidentally ran over the family cat and tears are streaming down their face.

The satisfaction you get from knowing you helped a less fortunate child get a new pair of shoes or a warm coat.

It's knowing that a parent trusts you enough with the care of their child to call and ask your opinion.

Sometimes it's the scared feeling you have for a child when you believe they are being neglected or abused, and there's nothing more you can do. Just being there and showing them you care can mean the world to them.

Offering encouraging words and prayers for those in need.

Cleaning and dressing a cut finger or burn on the people who prepare the breakfasts and lunches in the cafeteria.

Applying muscle rub to the janitors who pull and tug on the desk we want moved, or offering them anti-itch cream for the bug bites they get keeping our schoolyard mowed.

It's the pride you feel knowing you work in the school that won the clean and beautification award.

Being a Bulldog fan when you live in Blue Knight territory.

Enjoying lunch (when you finally get one) with friends.

Keeping your mouth shut and keeping the peace when all you really want to do is tell someone to SHUT UP!

It's knowing that I am making a difference by watching over the children and staff with the greatest of love to keep them happy, safe, and secure while at school.

Always being able to handle any health issues that occur and knowing I can ask for help if I'm overwhelmed and stressed out.

 It's having a big family who enriches my life and cares about me and shows me they care.

All this in a day's work of being a school nurse at Appalachia Elementary School, and loving every minute of it—good and bad. Every day that I work, I treat each task as a gift and a chance to demonstrate my skills. When things get tough and you want to give up, just look at the children whose lives you've touched. Thanks to AES I have fulfilled my dream of being able to help others.

Small Blessings

By Yvonne Elmore, RN, BSN

The public schools in El Paso, Texas were on a long Easter break in 1997. On a long-distance conversation with my Aunt Susan in California, she told me that her grandson, Brandon, was beginning to read.

"I can't wait until he's old enough to read to me the way his father did when he was a boy," she bubbled.

Those words made my heart ache. As a child, I once announced to a room full of my mother's friends that when I grew up, I was going to have one thousand children. At bedtime, I would tuck in every doll and stuffed animal in my bed until there was no room in it for me.

My first marriage produced no children. It ended in divorce after only three years when I was 34 years of age. Now, at 37, I was no closer to having the family I had always longed for.

After my divorce in 1994, I took a job in the Neonatal Intensive Care Unit of the hospital I had worked at before my marriage. Two years later, unsatisfied with my job, I took a position as a school nurse in the Ysleta Independent School District.

As a school nurse, I found that there was never time to sit down. Every morning, a steady stream of children paraded through my office until the dismissal bell. Tall piles of paperwork sat on every open space on my desk. I frequently stayed at school until 6:00 p.m. and came in on Saturdays to catch up with filing. But, I loved the kids and their parents, who let me know that I provided something no one else would fill. It was a decision I have never regretted.

On this Easter Sunday, however, I looked back at my career and my life. My failures seemed to weigh heavily. As I lay in bed at night, I thought about what my aunt had said. I imagined her holding her grandson, feeling his tender warmth while he read to her out loud. I mourned the loss of a child I knew might never be there. Tears welled in my eyes.

"God," I pleaded in frustration, "what have I done wrong? Why couldn't I have a little boy or girl to read to me?" That night, I cried myself to sleep.

The next morning I woke up tired. My irritability meant I was in for a rough day. The workload promised to be heavy as it always was after a long weekend. Immediately after the morning bell, my volunteer called to say she had a funeral to attend, and wouldn't be in to help.

Students flooded my office. Two students came in for each one who returned to class or went home. Some children stopped for sympathy for illnesses that had resolved during the holiday. Others asked for bandages for cuts too small to see with the naked eye. Most complained of generalized symptoms that disappeared as soon as they had someone to giggle with in the recovery area.

Every chair remained occupied, and all four beds were continually in use. As the hours ticked away, my frustration grew.

Finally, the office cleared and I found myself alone. I looked at the clock. 1:00 p.m. The school cafeteria had shut down— I had just missed lunch.

Oh well, I thought, *I'll use this time to tackle the letters that should have gone out days ago.*

I sat in my chair and put pen to paper, when I noticed out of the corner of my eye, a small boy standing in the doorway. Funny, I hadn't seen him walk in.

I looked at him over the top of my glasses. The boy, about 5 years old, had plump ruddy cheeks, full lips, and a mischievous look in his eyes. A mop of messy dark brown curls framed his face. He wore a dingy t-shirt. His jeans were faded, wrinkled, sported holes in both knees, and long strings trailed from the hems. He had apparently inherited them from an older brother.

As he stood on the threshold, he stared at me intently. He held both hands behind his back, and rocked rhythmically on the heels of his shoes. He didn't look sick or hurt. I waited for him to say something, but he was silent.

I put down my pen and sighed.

Probably another kid with another invisible boo-boo, I thought irritably.

"Well?" I asked, as I tried to hide my annoyance at the interruption. I waited. He didn't answer.

"What do you need?" I repeated.

The boy stopped rocking. In a very small voice, he whispered in Spanish, "I've been sent."

Sent? Sent to do what? Why don't they ever tell you the whole story, I thought.

With a gesture of my hand I urged him to continue talking. "Sent to do…*what?*" I asked.

The boy took a step toward me. From behind his back he brought out a small book and held it up for me to see.

"I've been sent to read to you," he whispered.

I was speechless. Tears came to my eyes. Without any invitation, the boy climbed on my lap and began to read to me. Over the next few minutes he read about a family of colorful clowns who all lived in harmony next door to each other. The sadness that drowned my soul the previous day evaporated in a single moment of time.

Later, the boy's teacher told me that she was sitting at her desk when she was suddenly inspired to send this student to the office to read to the principal. He ended up at my door by mistake.

I felt ashamed. While I wallowed in self-pity, a miracle was unfolding around me. Like Elias in the Bible, I had searched for answers in great events in my life and the big things in the world around me, only to discover the solution in a small voice.

I have never looked at my failures again the same way. When I drove home that day, I thanked God for answering my prayers. Now, I thank Him for the small blessings that surround me as they walk through the hallways of our school—all one thousand of them.

Caring for the Bird

By Maria Tela, RN

I never thought I would be a school nurse. I never thought I would be a nurse, period, but that's another story. I was a critical care nurse for many years, along with teaching nursing in colleges. I was looking for something new, when I learned of the opportunity to work in my children's elementary Montessori school. The small, private school had never had a nurse and so there was a need, not only for a nurse, but also to begin a nursing program!

I applied and was hired, and set about the business of learning to be a school nurse. It was difficult. What I found the most difficult was the isolation. When I worked in the hospital, I had unlimited resources at my fingertips. Sure, the patients were very sick and complicated, but I had support. I had help. I worked at teaching hospitals, where the interns and residents were a few steps away at all times. We had respiratory therapists, pharmacists, laboratory technicians, and so on—all available to help the nurses care for their patients. While students in the schools weren't this sick, there weren't many resources, either. I spent a lot of time visiting other nurses in other schools and getting valuable information from them. Eventually I set up my program, and I felt, after a few years, that I was learning how to be a school nurse.

I had students from nursing schools come and visit the school. I wanted them to see this wonderful profession of school nursing that is so understated, and yet, so rewarding.

Although nurses can make far more money in a hospital or other acute care setting, there are benefits and rewards to being a school nurse. Having all summer off is a great benefit, as is not having to work weekends, nights, or holidays. And I loved the children. Half the students in my school are under the age of six. It's a great place, and I feel that I've learned a lot, that I've never stopped learning. I've come to rely on other school nurses in nearby schools, as well as the teachers, staff, and administration in my school for support.

"I take care of everyone," I would tell the nursing students. It's not just the students of the school who come to me, but sometimes the teachers need care, too. I've had to care for visitors to the school as well; if they are here and have a medical need, they come to the school nurse.

My job is varied and interesting, and I feel like I have to know a little bit about everything. Still, nothing ever prepared me for the day the kindergarten teacher came to me with a little bird in her hand. She had a pair of parakeets that had been donated to the school by a family. She'd had the birds for a while, these silly, cute little parakeets that livened up the classroom with their songs and chatter.

One bird was now sick. He looked horrible when she brought him to me. She said he wasn't perching, but was on the bottom of the cage. Now, I'm an animal lover, and I've had many birds in my life, and I know that not perching is a bad sign. *Still,* I thought, *maybe we can help him.* I took the bird, because she didn't want to keep him in the cage with all the children there. I put him in a little box, and lined it with soft cloth to keep him comfortable and warm. Every now and then, he'd perk up, and I'd think *Maybe he's not so bad.*

One of the directors came to my office, saw the bird, and immediately she felt for him. The parakeet was such a cute little thing, fluffy, white with bluish markings. We wanted to help him, but we didn't know how. We decided keeping him secure and warm was a plus. Then, we thought maybe we could get some food or water into him. He felt kind of skinny, but, then, birds aren't really ever fat. Maybe he just needed some hydration. We made a concoction of water and sugar, and I got one of my disposable medication droppers to feed him. He seemed to like the water, and drank some of it, keeping it down. We decided not to keep him in my office, after all, I had children coming in and out, and I didn't think it would be a good idea to keep a sick bird there.

The director brought the bird and his box to her desk, and she took care of him, talking to him, and stroking him. Every now and then, we held him and he would perch. This encouraged us, thinking it was a good sign. But the bird failed to make any other progress, and he didn't look comfortable, so I decided that I would bring the bird to my veterinarian after school.

"You'll probably have to pay for the visit," the teacher warned, and I said I didn't care; I couldn't stand to see the bird suffer any longer. He looked at me with his little black eyes, and I could tell that he wasn't feeling well, and wanted me to help him. This went on for a few hours, and finally, school finished. I bundled his box up and drove him to my vet. The vet examined him, and shook his head.

"Feel this," he told me, and I felt by his gullet, which was soft and squishy. "Feels like a beanbag, right?" he asked.

"Yes. It does."

"It's seeds."

"What?" I didn't understand.

"It's seeds," he repeated. "He has some sort of blockage, probably a tumor. It's not allowing the seeds to go down, and they're all backing up in there. Birds can store some seeds there, but not like this."

I looked at the poor bird, and couldn't imagine the pain he must have been in. He was failing, too, I could see that. He was getting weaker and his breathing had changed. Basically, he was starving to death.

"What should we do?" I asked, but even as I asked, I knew the answer.

"Well, if he was my bird," the doctor said, "I would put him to sleep."

I hated thinking about this. I hated doing this. He wasn't even my bird.

"I, uh, can I call the school?" I asked.

"Of course," he said, and stepped out to give me a few minutes to make my decision. I called the teacher, who told me she trusted me to make the right decision.

"Okay," I said. "I think I have to do this. He's really suffering."

The bird started arching his back in a way I'd never seen before. I said goodbye to the little bird, and then, the vet took him away. He came back a few moments later.

"It's done," he said.

I can't imagine how they would euthanize a bird, and I didn't really want to know. *At least the bird was at peace now,* I thought. I felt badly for him, for the suffering he'd gone through, and the fact that he had to be put to sleep. But I felt I'd made the right decision, the only decision that could be made. I took the little body back in his box, and the director and I buried the bird outside in the garden.

That happened last year. I can still look out my window and see the area where he was buried. It was an experience that bothered me, and I shared it with my fellow teachers and family. I know he was "just a bird" and wasn't even my bird. But he was a life, and he was in pain, and it's funny that the teacher thought to bring the bird to me, the school nurse. But maybe it's not so funny after all. I'm here, as all the school nurses are, to care for people that are sick, in pain, or just in need of a human touch. And that can extend to other creatures as well.

Not only do I take care of students, teachers, and visitors, but I've taken care of the bird, too. It's added another dimension to my nursing experience, and especially, to my school nursing experience. In nursing, anything can happen, and I feel that this experience is a testimony to that.

IV.

Easing the Pain of Troubled Children

*"I am reminded once again
that the job of school nurse
is so much more than just
putting bandages on scraped knees."*

–Frances Harmon, RN, BSN, PHN

Ice Pack Molly

By Kerry E. Warren, RN

It was the first day of school and my office looked as if a whirling dervish had just blown through. I had already spent two weeks at school sorting through physicals, dental forms, and medication permission slips. Now I had students and parents lined up at my door. Most of these visits were routine and my morning sped by.

However, just before lunch, a new sixth grade student stopped by. She sat quietly in a chair.

"Dear," I said, "if you're not feeling well, please gel up your hands and write your name on the clipboard." She dutifully walked to my desk, applied hand sanitizer, and wrote her name. Although it was difficult to read, I made out the letters M-O-L-L-Y. No last name.

"May I take your temperature? What's hurting?" I asked. "I'd like an ice pack, please. My wrist hurts," Molly replied.

I handed her the ice pack, but she was unable to tell me why her wrist hurt. I explained to Molly how an ice pack can help an injury and asked her to return it when she was finished with it.

Two weeks into school and the initial wave of paperwork had ebbed. I could see the top of my desk and most of the student files were in the filing cabinets. I could breathe again. Molly stopped by my office, "gelled" up her hands, and signed in. She waited quietly for her turn.

"I have a headache," Molly stated.

I took her temperature. No fever.

"Would you like me to call someone to see if they can bring you something?" I asked.

"No one is at home," Molly replied.

"I could give you an ice pack," I stated. Molly agreed. "Hold it against your forehead. It will constrict some of the blood vessels," I explained. I demonstrated constriction with my hand.

It was now the end of September and I had to begin vision screenings. How was I going to juggle 400 vision screenings in the next few weeks in addition to my regular responsibilities? In order to maintain some level of order in my office I knew that I needed to complete the screenings before the flu season started.

By now, Molly was a regular feature in my office. Her symptoms were always vague and her ailments always minor: a stubbed toe, a stuffy nose, a scraped knee, a scratchy throat. Molly didn't say much to me, but she was always polite. The ice packs, the bandages, and the saltwater gargles were always accompanied by a brief lesson on treatments, cures, and preventions. I took the teaching aspect of my job as a school nurse very seriously.

Thanksgiving break was coming up. I was beginning to see higher fevers, redder throats, and deeper coughs. I was really glad I completed those vision screenings. Molly came into my office complaining of a stuffy head. No fever.

"For the next three days I want you to drink until you float," I said to Molly. She looked at me with a quizzical expression on her face.

"Molly, I want you to drink and drink and drink. All of that extra fluid will help your head drain," I instructed.

"Okay," she said as she headed back to class. I wondered to myself *Am I wasting my breath as I go through these instructions?*

Our two week holiday break couldn't come soon enough. I was sending home at least a dozen sick students each day.

Molly's visits continued. Oddly enough, I never sent her home. It was unlikely, but perhaps she liked my company. The holiday break finally arrived. I didn't know who needed it more, the staff or the students.

We returned to school in January adorned with new hats, new mufflers, and new red noses. My office seemed to use a box of tissues per day. Molly stopped by requesting an ice pack.

"What happened?" I asked, more out of habit than true concern at this point.

"I slipped and fell as I got off the bus," she replied. I checked her palm, which she had extended. No visible injury. She left with an ice pack.

I began all of my hearing screenings in February. At least I could spread these over a couple of months. I could easily accommodate two or three students a day. The paperwork usually had to get done after school. I saw Molly several times over the next few weeks: another bumped elbow, a minor stomachache, a tickle in her throat.

March arrived, but the cold, damp weather refused to leave. On the way to school I saw a robin and couldn't help but wonder if he would survive the freezing temperatures. My mind was wandering to Spring Break chores and tulips when I glanced up and noticed my office was almost full. Molly sat among the other students. As I tended to students with P.E. injuries and high fevers, I told Molly that she would have to wait patiently. She didn't complain. After phoning a few parents and sending the remaining students back to class, Molly said she had something to tell me. I headed to the freezer to grab an ice pack. Molly shook her head.

"I don't need an ice pack," she said. "I just wanted to tell you that today is my last day; my family is moving."

I was stunned. Couldn't her family wait until the end of the school year or at least until the end of the grading period?

"But I'll try to remember what you taught me," Molly stated.

"Did I teach you something?" I asked.

"Yes, you taught me to drink a lot when I have a stuffy nose and to gargle warm saltwater when my throat is scratchy," Molly replied.

"I'm really happy you remembered all of that," I said. I pulled an ice pack from the freezer and wrote 'Good Luck' on it with a marker.

"Molly, I think you deserve your very own ice pack," I stated. "I hope you enjoy your new school."

As she headed toward the door of my office, another student entered.

"I just jammed my finger. I think I need an ice pack," he said, trying to hold back tears. Molly turned around just long enough to say, "It'll constrict the blood vessels and that will keep the swelling down."

The remainder of the school year was a little lonely without Molly. I secretly wished that her family would move back to our community. I thought to myself *Molly taught me a lot during our seven months together.* She never let on that she truly understood any of my instructions, but now I know she listened to every word I said.

Oh, Those Horrible Headaches!

By Julia Plaut, RN, BSN

Last year I had a 6th grade student, John, who was suffering from severe and frequent headaches. He was visiting the clinic from one to three times a day. OTC pain relievers weren't helping. The parents had consulted their pediatrician, who then referred them to a neurologist and an ophthalmologist. John had a CT scan done with negative findings. The ophthalmologist prescribed eyeglasses for him and said his vision was severely compromised in his left eye. They thought his vision deficit might be the cause of his headaches. Unfortunately, John found no relief, even with his prescribed glasses.

John was missing a lot of class time, from resting in the clinic or going home. His neurologist prescribed migraine headache medication, but it didn't work either. It made him sleepy, so he'd fall asleep at home or in my office. Being new to the school and to me, I had asked John and his parents if anything was going on in class that might be upsetting him emotionally. They had said, "No." We consulted with his teachers, and they were not aware of any academic or social problems at school. The parents said that John was not a complainer. John was in pain most of the time, and he was giving up. His parents were at their wits' end. They hated to see their vibrant child in pain and sleepy from medications that were not helping him.

I had been reading up on "upper cervical chiropractic," where the chiropractor adjusts the axis and/or atlas bones at the base of the skull. This type of chiropractor has further specialized training in order to manipulate the bones at the C1 and C2 level painlessly and with ease. If those two tiny bones are out of place, they will throw the rest of the spine out of alignment, which puts pressure on nerves and vessels. Many times with young children, falling off of bikes and skateboards can cause those bones to misalign, which creates problems that develop later on. This type of chiropractic care made sense to me, and I made an appointment with the Upper Cervical Chiropractor to learn more about this type of care, and how it could help some of my friends, family, and middle school students. After speaking with the doctor, I was convinced that this type of care would be beneficial for certain conditions.

I discussed what I learned about upper cervical chiropractic with John's parents. They were willing to give it a try, because the traditional treatment modes were not working. They had a consult with Dr. L., and he saw that John's atlas/axis was misaligned. The misalignment may have contributed to his vision decline in his left eye. After John had a thorough history and assessment, they remembered that he crashed while riding his bike over the summer. This accident may have caused the misalignment and the resulting headaches.

After several adjustments, John's headaches improved, and he was spending less time in the clinic and more time in class. John continued with his adjustments over the summer. When I saw him at the beginning of this school year, I asked him how his headaches were doing. He hugged me with a big smile on his face and said that he hardly ever got headaches anymore. This case has taught me that persistence and opening up your mind to new treatment modalities found relief for this child!

Stop!

By Frances Harmon, RN, BSN, PHN

Dear Dad,

I am so upset with the events of today. I am not sure that writing to you will be able to help calm my troubled heart. In the past, writing to you has helped to provide me with peace of mind and has even helped me find answers to troubling questions. I can only hope this letter will do the same for me now.

The seasonal cold and flu viruses have begun to make their rounds just in time for Christmas vacation. Our office has been filled with children coughing, sneezing, throwing up, and running to the bathroom. In other words, we have been up to our gills in bodily fluids!

It frustrates me to no end when a child is sent to school when they are still hacking and sneezing! While a parent may think it is "just a cold," their child *should* stay at home until they are well so they don't contaminate the world.

I am always concerned that a child with a "simple" cold will expose themselves to a teacher or student (or school nurse!) who has a compromised immune system and *that* poor person will end up with pneumonia or worse! Anyways, I will get off of my soapbox for this subject and move on to what happened today.

For some reason, today was a particularly bad day. We were up to our armpits in sick kids. Some children were waiting outside for their parents to pick them up while others were waiting to be examined to see if they should be sent home. I had just gotten off the phone with one parent when Sally came in.

Sally is a really exceptional child, very mature for her age—sort of an "old soul." She is sweet and always looking out for her classmates. She is very polite and tries to always be of assistance to others. She is also very smart.

Today, she came in and told me she was sick. I went through the usual line of questioning.

"What do you mean 'sick'? Can you describe what you are feeling?" I asked her.

"My stomach is upset. I feel like I am going to throw up!" explained Sally.

I was about to begin my assessment when I was called away by a child who was obviously about to lose their lunch. When I returned Sally was gone and a note from her teacher was left on my desk.

The note read "I have taken Sally back to class. She has been fine all day. She has to take a spelling test today. I think she is just trying to avoid the test."

This just wasn't like Sally! I was concerned that something may be wrong. I contacted her mother and told her of my concern. The mother confirmed my belief that something was wrong with Sally, but it was more than just an upset stomach.

Several weeks ago, Sally made a mistake during a spelling bee. One of her classmates started to tease Sally by calling her "stupid" and a "loser." Then Sally started finding cruel notes in her book bag and lunch box. The other children started to tease her and exclude her from games. Sally's grades started to drop. Her mother believed Sally's upset stomach was caused by the fear of failing and the stress from being bullied.

As you can imagine, I discussed the issue with Sally's teacher and with the school counselor. Once they became aware of the problem, both the teacher and the counselor began to work with Sally and addressed the issue of bullying with the class.

I wish I could say this is the only case of bullying I have faced this year, but sadly it isn't. I have had several children come in to see me because they had "upset stomachs." After speaking with them I would discover they were anxious and sad because they were being bullied.

I know bullying has been around since the beginning of time, but that doesn't make it right. We have gone to war to fight "bullies," to fight against prejudices and, yet, it has reached epidemic levels within our own schools.

I am sure you can imagine all the theories that have come out in an attempt to explain why bullying seems to be on the rise. Some believe it is the music our children listen to or the shows they watch. Granted, there was a cult that seemed to take their lead from a cartoon character that bullied people with brown eyes. And, yes, there were several children who seemed to follow what they perceived to be "instructions" from the lyrics of a song when they decided to bring guns to school and shoot anyone in their path. But, I can't help but think there is more to it than just cartoons and lyrics.

Each time the news reports the suicide of a bullied child, or the attack of a child by a mob led by a bully, there is a surge of people that cry out, "We must have a zero tolerance on bullying within our schools!" And yet, the bullying continues.

Dad, I remember when I had a problem with being bullied when I was in high school. I was singled out because I was rather small for my age. The bigger kids would pick me up, toss me as if I was a rag doll, and destroy my homework and books.

I remember how I dreaded going to school and how I was constantly looking over my shoulder. I remember having to run to safety when the big kids saw me and started chasing me. It was horrible! But I also remember what you told me when I came to you for help. It was so simple.

"Stop."

Do you remember telling me that?! You said, "Just stop. Stop running. Stop giving them your power. Just stop."

The next day, when the bullies saw me and started chasing me, I remembered what you had said. When they picked me up and threw me against the wall, I told them with a voice of authority that came from some unknown place deep inside me, *"Leave me alone!"* Before I knew it, they just put me down, laughed, and walked off. They never bothered me again.

Dad, I don't know if people will ever be able to see that we are all responsible for creating an environment where bullying is acceptable. We send mixed signals to our children when we laugh at shows that make light of bullying in the workplace and home. We demand the schools take action and yet we fail to realize that the lessons of "Bullying 101" are not taught at school.

I know! I know! I can almost hear you say the words "It is the parent's job to teach their child to respect all creatures and to hold their child accountable for their actions! It is the parent's job to teach their child that they have the ability to stop the bullying by just not giving up their power to the bully." Yes, yes, "sticks and stones may break my bones but names can never hurt me...unless I allow them to!"

I know that saying is true. Whether we are 5 or 55, the instant we give the power of our spirit to a bully, they win. As soon as we allow ourselves to believe what they say about us, we lose the ability to see ourselves for who we really are and who we have the potential to be.

Unfortunately, I know I will see more children like Sally who are bullied by their classmates. I am reminded once again that the job of the school nurse is so much more than just putting bandages on scraped knees. It is also listening carefully to determine what the real problem is, and to try to provide comfort when the soul has been bruised. It is giving a child a gentle reminder that they do have the power to just say, "Stop!"

They have the ability to keep their power or to give it away to the bullies.

Once again, you have helped me sort things out.

Thank you, Dad! Thank you for being brave enough to not always give me what I wanted, but always giving me what I needed. For teaching me to respect all creatures "great and small," and for holding me accountable for my actions. Thank you for teaching me to just "stop" and never give away my power to bullies.

As always, I love you and miss you.
Marie

It Takes a Village

By Janett Doile, RN

John was a gentle giant. He was a high school student of large stature with a mature, quiet nature. He played football and was quite a successful wrestler in the heavyweight division. I first encountered him the fall of his sophomore year. He came in from the football practice field with suspicious small pustules on his arms and hands. I told him he needed to see a doctor, but he informed me he did not have one.

During the course of our conversation, his dreadful home life was revealed. He had been in a foster home that no longer felt able to care for him. There was no father in his life. His mother was a low-functioning woman barely able to care for herself. He had a grandfather in another town that he stayed with "sometimes." Presently, he was staying with friends. This was his first year of attending school in our town. I called a doctor and got him an appointment that very afternoon. His diagnosis was a staph infection for which an antibiotic was prescribed. Through a donated fund, I was able to pay for the doctor's office visit and the medication.

A year later, again during football, John began visiting my health office quite frequently. His complaint was usually "not feeling well," often with a sore throat. He said he was feeling tired and run-down. Occasionally he would have a low-grade fever of 99–100. At one time he was taking an antibiotic, so I thought he was under the care of a physician. His home situation had not improved and he was still staying with friends, only now he was shuffling around amongst his friends, staying a week here and a week there.

It was obvious to me this young man needed a lot of help, but I was concerned that we first needed to understand what was interfering with his physical health. He had no physician, no health insurance, or state aid. Again, I called on the same local physician who had previously helped John.

After football practice John kept his appointment and by evening he was in a hospital in a nearby larger city with the diagnosis of leukemia. John would be able to return to school while taking chemotherapy. Oncology nurses came to our school and visited with teachers, coaches, staff members, and students to help us respond appropriately. Our school was tremendous in supporting and helping John. He was allowed to wear a stocking cap to cover his baldness. His schedule was adjusted to accommodate his medical appointments, treatments, and energy level. One coach stepped forward and gave him a permanent home. He was assisted in applying for state aid to help with medical bills. The ladies in the office made a Christmas gift of a letter jacket to John, who would never have been able to purchase one on his own. I'll never forget the big, silent tears rolling down his face when he first put on that letter jacket. It was his only coat.

Our school communicated with his grandfather, who took a more active role in John's life even though he could not care for him full time. We visited with his mother, who was able to see John from time to time.

John missed his junior year of wrestling and his senior year of football, but was able to wrestle again his senior year. What a courageous kid! Our entire school was proud and full of emotion when he graduated!

The saying "It takes a village to raise a child" was certainly true in this case. As a school nurse, you don't have to do it all or do it alone, just get the ball rolling and call on available resources. Sometimes a group just needs a leader and a direction to make a positive difference for young people like John.

He Needed to Talk

By Vicki Senter, RN

He entered my high school nursing office as so many students do, and sat down in the waiting area. I got up from my desk and asked what was wrong. The young man stated he was sent out of class "because the teacher is an idiot." After a few more questions, he admitted he was not paying attention, and had laid his head on the desk. I reminded him that when a student gets sent out of class he needs to go to the main office, not the nurse's office. The student said he knew that, but he didn't want to sit in the main office for the rest of the period. He spent many classes in the main office for various reasons. I told him he really needed to go to the main office.

He didn't move. He remained seated on the sick bed across from my desk. His head was bent down as he looked at his hands. Because of the expression on his face, I asked if something else was wrong. He stated that he was missing Brad. Brad was a student in our school who passed away when he was hit by a car while riding his bicycle. It was devastating to our entire high school and community.

I said, "I know, I miss him too." He stated he dreamt about Brad the previous night. I asked what the dream was about. The young man got very serious as he told me that Brad had come to visit him. Brad looked the same as he always did. He was wearing the zip-up hooded gray sweatshirt he always wore. He had a smile on his face from ear to ear. He bummed a cigarette and said something else. It bothered this student that he couldn't remember what Brad had said to him. He said Brad was mumbling like he usually did, and he couldn't understand what Brad was saying. I asked what he thought Brad would have said to him if he was there. This brought a big smile to his face. He thought Brad would have told him to "smarten up."

This student had been skipping classes, something that Brad seldom did. We talked about this for the remainder of the period. We talked about Brad and how he always came to school. How Brad wasn't the best student; he never did homework, and was often late to class. But you could count on Brad to be at school every day. His smile and laugh would always cheer you up.

I checked this young man's attendance later and noted he had been skipping school. I did not refer him to the main office. I notified his teacher that he was with me and that he needed to be with me. He received no discipline for the events of that day.

Even the "trouble makers" need someone to talk to from time to time. They are not the students who will go to their guidance counselor and ask for assistance. They are too cool. They have it all together. They can handle anything. They are tough. They are the ones who will leave class without permission. They are the ones who punch walls and lockers. They are the ones who don't know what to do with their feelings. Sometimes the toughest kids are the ones who are searching for and need the most help.

I checked his attendance a month later. He hadn't missed a single day.

V.

The Day-to-Day Life of a School Nurse

"…a second spent with a child is never insignificant."

–Ann Ellington, RN

My First Year
as a School Nurse

By Liz Missildine, RN

My school nurse career began in 2010. Previously, I worked in clinical settings. I am now a nurse in an early childhood center with 200 four-year-old Pre-K and Head Start children. In the year I have been here, I have enjoyed this job so much more than my previous jobs! Every child is a reward and a joy. We had a "Meet the Teachers" night and I stayed to help out. When a child introduced me to his parents, he would say, "This is our doctor and her office." So cute and serious they all are!

The first week of school went very well. It was still summer, without a lot of illness going around. I saw a few students in my office for headaches and asthma, along with a lot of playground scratches on knees and elbows. Occasionally I would treat a few bumped heads with knots popping out. These sorts of injuries continued for about three weeks.

One day I was sitting at my desk, immersed in reviewing immunization records. The morning had been quiet, without any students visiting for injury or illness. The excitement began in the late morning, around 11:00 a.m., with a teacher bringing a student to my office. The student had fallen, hitting her mouth on a desk in the classroom. At first glance, I remembered the saying "A teaspoon of blood in the toilet looks like a pint." The student had blood running down her chin, onto her clothing, and into her hands. She was terrified—crying and whimpering. My adrenaline started pumping as I grabbed a change of clothes and towels. I began to treat the area. Upon further inspection, I saw that she had bitten through her bottom lip. As I finished cleaning her up and calling her mother, another teacher arrived with student number two.

"What is the problem?" I asked.

The teacher answered, "This child has eaten a mushroom that was growing on the playground."

One of the other teachers told her it might be poisonous, because it was white with black underneath. The little girl was just adorable, with beautiful black eyes and long black pigtails in her hair. She was absolutely horrified because she overheard the teachers on the playground discussing the potential poisonous nature of the mushroom. I immediately called the student's doctor, who said she should be taken to the emergency room immediately. He continued to explain that she might hallucinate as a result of eating the mushroom. I quickly called her mother, and sent the teacher outside for a sample of the suspected mushrooms to take to the hospital for diagnosis.

While waiting on the mushroom eater's mother to arrive, two children with headaches but without fever entered the health office. After assessment, I called each child's parents; one student was sent home, and the other back to lunch. I checked on my mushroom eater. She had not started to hallucinate, however, her eyes were beginning to look a little "fuzzy" and dilated. After 30 minutes of waiting, her mother arrived to take her to the emergency room. Without a moment's pause, another teacher arrived with a child who had received ant bites all over her legs, and was dancing about the office from the itching. As she began to break out in a rash, I called her parents to receive permission to administer medication. Luckily the reaction was not accompanied by shortness of breath, so I did not need to call 9-1-1. The ant bite student's mother was on the way!

As soon as that student was settled, another child with a rash appeared in my doorway. His rash was around his mouth, presumably from something he ate. I first checked for breathing problems—thankfully, he had none. Not missing a beat, I called his parents to report the reaction. This mother opted to allow her son to remain in school until the end of the day. After the mouth-rash student was sent back to class, a child with vomiting and severe stomachache entered the office!

With that, the parade of illness and injury into my office came to a pause. I realized that I did not eat lunch. As I heard the final bell ring, I stared at the clock. How did it get to be 3:00 p.m. already? I sat back in my chair and laughed out loud. What a day—I love this job!

The mushroom eater was hospitalized overnight, and her stomach was pumped. The little girl with the hole in her lip went to the emergency room, but did not need stitches. The student with ant bites was given antihistamines and attended school the next day, as did the other children I sent home that day.

I never thought I would be dealing with so much back-to-back trauma in one day! Somehow, I survived that first year (although I hope I never repeat that day), and truly love my new job as a school nurse!

The Miracle

By Kyra Manry, RN

One fall day I was just about to sit down and have a nice
lunch, or so I thought, when the clinic door opened and a teacher
and two students entered. One student had a large hematoma
on her head and felt "kind of dizzy." I did a quick assessment
of the head wound and asked the teacher to get an ice pack,
as the other student needed my immediate attention. The left
side of the young man's forehead was bleeding profusely, his
left eye was full of glass particles, and his right wrist "really
hurt bad."

The students had just pulled out of our student parking lot
on a drizzly, rainy day when the car she was driving slipped off
the road and into a utility pole across the street. She had had
her seat belt on and hit her head hard enough for a bump and
concussion. He, however, did not have his seat belt on, and he
slid forward, hitting the windshield hard. He said he threw
up his right arm to try to protect his face from the force of the
cracking windshield.

First I gloved up and started gathering supplies, including a
large bottle of sterile water, and a whole jar of gauze. I flushed
the head wound and applied pressure and a dressing to stop
the bleeding. Then I took the exam light and checked his left
eye. I could see glass particles in his eye. I flushed his eye over
and over again as I asked him to look at different areas of the
room until all the eye solution was gone. I believe it was 500 to
600 cc's worth of fluid.

I knew I had to keep washing the eye until I did not see any more glass, or until he did not feel any more glass in his eye. Then I checked out his right wrist; it was swollen, hurting, he was having trouble moving it, and he had limited range of motion. I grabbed a splint board, rolls of gauze, and medical tape, and supported the wrist to the board with gauze. I applied a large bag of ice and wrapped it securely with more gauze. By this time the paramedics arrived, and the girl's parents showed up to take her to the doctor.

The male student came back about a week later with a gauze bandage encircling his head and left eye, and a cast on his right wrist. He said he just wanted to thank me for helping him that day, because they told him in the emergency room that because I flushed out his eye so well, I probably saved the vision in that eye. He also said he broke his right wrist when he hit the windshield. I know having a Registered Nurse on campus, ready to act right away, made a big difference in his life.

Are You a Nurse?

By Lorali Gray, RN, BSN, M. Ed, NCSN

It was Halloween and I was scheduled to work at the high school. Past practice allowed for students and staff to dress up as long as it did not "disrupt the educational process." I had never dressed up before, and decided this year I would do it right: I would be a registered nurse. I dug out my old traditional nursing uniform (that had not seen the light of day in years): white slacks and tunic, white knee highs, white shoes, and of course, my nursing cap. To dress it up I donned every nursing pin and health and wellness button I could find—it was Halloween after all. They covered the entire front of my uniform and included "I Got My Flu Shot Did You?", "Don't Judge a Vegetable by its Cover", "Proud to be Smoke Free", and even a flashing strobe heart pin. To top it off, I hung my stethoscope around my neck and clipped my penlight to my front pocket.

I was looking forward to the day as I approached the campus; however, when I walked into the main office I knew something was askew. It quickly became apparent that no one was wearing a costume, not even a pumpkin necklace! "Where are your costumes?" I whispered to one of the secretaries. "Oh, the administration decided that it was too disruptive so we can't wear them this year," she replied. As we talked I could feel all eyes on me and my white uniform. I went into the health room and quickly closed the door. Off came the cap, the plethora of pins, buttons, and stethoscope. I had a sweater I kept on hand, put it over my tunic, and buttoned it up. That would just have to do, I thought. After all, I really am a nurse and this uniform represented a profession of which I am proud.

During the course of the day, necessity required that I forget about my "costume" in order to take care of the crises at hand. At some point I began to take note of the reactions and comments from students around me.

"Are you a nurse?" a student asked as he walked by.

Hmmm, I thought, *I had been his school nurse since he was in kindergarten, about 10 years now!* I wondered who he thought I had been all those years. Another student coming in for their lunchtime medication stood next to me eyeing my unusual dress.

"Wow, what a lot of white you are wearing; nurses don't dress like that anymore do they? Are you a real nurse?"

This raised an even more important question. How many other students did not know that I was their school nurse? Had something been lost when nurses gave up the white uniform? An identity, an image? An image that has gotten lost in a world of modern day nursing, especially in a school setting where it is more student-friendly to dress without the whites, uniform, or lab coat? Yet clearly more than one student acknowledged this white uniform to be that of a professional nurse. Clearly more than one student recognized the powerful image this uniform portrayed: nurses are valued and trusted professionals. Although to "stand apart" was not what I expected that day, I was reminded that it was my uniform that allowed me to "stand apart" as a readily identifiable nurse.

While the wearing of this uniform started out as a Halloween costume, it ended up as it truly was and should be, representing the image of a profession—the most trusted profession in the nation. It was through that uniform I was sending a powerful message to all the students in my care: I am your professional school nurse.

The Lesson

By Patricia VanHavermaat, BSN, RN, NCSN

It had been a particularly busy, trying Friday in my middle school nurse's office; a challenge to say the least. Two boys in particular had been very rude, crude, and difficult. Even so, I did the best I could for them. After they left my office, I thought about their inappropriate behavior. No matter how kindly I cared for their needs, they had continued their offensive conduct. I made the decision to call their parents and let them know what had happened, and ask for their support by letting their sons know that this behavior was unacceptable.

After the final bell I called the first parent, who agreed to speak to his son. I then called the second parent and related what had happened. He was very supportive, and said he would also speak to his son. Both said I should expect an apology on Monday. As I had never called a parent for this reason before, I felt badly about it, and hoped I would never have to do it again.

Monday came and so did one apology, after which my student and I discussed what we both could have done to make a difference regarding his behavior on Friday. Afterwards, we shook hands and he went to class. I thought *One out of two ain't so bad,* and got busy with my day. About mid-morning, one of the office secretaries called and asked if I was aware that the father of one of our students had committed suicide on Saturday. I asked who the student was and discovered it was the father of the student who had not come to apologize.

I felt horrible. With a lot of negative self-talk, I convinced myself I was partly responsible—that my call to this father on Friday was quite possibly the last straw, and suicide was his chosen method of dealing with it. Was this rational? Of course not!

By this time, I had a few years under my belt as a school nurse and had dealt with many tragic and sad situations. This one ranked right up there and I didn't seem to be able to get past it. I grieved for my student and for his father.

The student did not return to school. He moved to another town to be with his mother. As the days passed, the father's suicide was the talk of the community. I finally began to realize that my call had nothing to do with his death. I no longer felt like the match that lit the fire. I did, however, learn a valuable lesson.

The lesson I learned was simple: sometimes when a student acts out, there may be a deeper reason than what appears on the surface. I think I always knew this, but had lost sight of it on that particular exhausting day ten years ago. One just never knows what happens in the life of a student away from school. In school nursing, as in life, the lessons are there; they need to be embraced and remembered. I know I will never forget this particular lesson.

A Cheerful Giver

By Janett Doile, RN

One year I took it upon myself to update the health offices in my district. I started my project with new bedding for the existing cots. Because of my budget restrictions, I spent my free time at local auctions and garage sales, as well as asking the school staff if they had items to donate.

While working on the updating, I told each student who stopped in my office about the project. One day, a fifth grade girl walked into my office. She said her family had just redesigned her bedroom, and there was a twin-size comforter that was no longer needed. She wanted to know if I could use it in my redecorating project. I was thrilled with her offer! I had never thought of involving the students, but here was proof that they wanted to help.

I cheerfully accepted the little pink, blue, and yellow comforter. I asked the small donor where she would prefer to have her comforter end up. She shyly replied that it did not matter, but she would be happy if it stayed at her grade school. So, I proudly displayed that little pink, blue, and yellow comforter in the school where the cheerful giver attended. That inspirational young lady has since gone on to middle school, but that bright little spread is still in her grade school.

The Door with a "C" (Clinic)

By Anetta K. Flowers-Moreaux, RN, BSN

The clinic is not just a name; rather, it's the staff which infuses the people it serves with love, power, knowledge, and a sense of community. The C is symbolic and focuses on all the clinic has to offer.

Starting school can be a frightening experience for most boys and girls: meeting other children, learning different things, and being in new places. Jason Jones was no exception.

"Mommy, what time does school start?" asked Jason.

"It starts at 7:30 a.m. so get in the car or we will be late," replied Jason's mom. "I cannot wait to see all the wonderful places in your school," she said.

When they arrived, Jason eagerly showed his mom the library, cafeteria, gym, and his classroom.

"Jason, what about the door over there?" asked his mom.

"I am afraid of that door," said Jason. "The boys and girls I see walking through that door are crying, coughing, and complaining. I do not know what happens once they get inside. Mom, when you were in school, did you ever go through the door with the C?" whispered Jason.

"You mean the clinic? Oh yes. The clinic is a good place to get help when you do not feel well. The nurse and aide are really friendly, caring, and helpful. They give medicines and special treatments, and provide information regarding vaccinations, places to receive glasses, hearing and vision testing, and other helpful things to make you feel better," replied Jason's mom.

"My teacher, Ms. Dugan, says that we will be visiting the clinic next week and I am scared! Nobody ever looks happy when they go there!" cried Jason.

"Try not to worry, maybe you should talk to a friend or your teacher, and find out how they feel about the door with the C," said Jason's mom.

"I'll do that tomorrow!" proclaimed Jason.

The next day, Jason asked his best friend Michael if he was afraid of going into the door with the C. "I love the nurse!" exclaimed Michael. "She fixes my ouches, lets me rest when my tummy is hurting, gives me big hugs, and you can get great stickers when you leave," chuckled Michael.

"Stickers? Wow, I love stickers!" shouted Jason.

When the morning started, Jason approached his teacher and said "Good morning, Ms. Dugan. Can I ask you a question?"

"Yes, Jason what is it?" replied Ms. Dugan.

"Have you visited the door with the C?" he asked.

"What door are you talking about?" responded Ms. Dugan.

Jason pointed at the door he had feared.

"Oh, that door," said Ms. Dugan. "Yes, the clinic staff helps everyone whenever there is a need. Also, the nurse is a great listener. You can share your feelings about school, sports, hobbies, and other cool things with the nurse. Having a clinic inside the school is a very good thing," explained Ms. Dugan.

"It sounds like the clinic is not a yucky place, but a good one," said Jason.

"Maybe if you go inside, it won't be so scary," suggested Ms. Dugan.

Jason considered this, then walked over to the door with the C. He peeked through a crack, when suddenly the nurse opened the door.

"May I help you?" asked the nurse.

"I just want to see what goes on inside this door!" uttered Jason.

"Well, come on in and find out," said the nurse.

The nurse told Jason that her job is to care for the children when they become sick or hurt, give medications when needed, check students' vision and/or hearing, listen to problems, and try to help parents keep them healthy.

"So...what you are saying is that I can just come in here to talk with you even if I am not sick or hurt?" asked Jason.

"That's right," said the nurse. Then she handed him two stickers.

"Wow, thanks!" exclaimed Jason. "Now I am not afraid anymore; this is really a good place."

Jason smiled and sighed as he exited the door with the C. "The door with the C is really cool," laughed Jason.

The Joy of Clean Clothes

By Lorraine Watkins, RN

It was my second year as the school nurse of a busy elementary school in the suburbs of Charlotte, North Carolina. One fall day, a sweet little girl came to me for a change of clothes, as she had gotten paint on her dress. It is a rare day that I don't see a child in need of a change of clothes. Usually, they gladly change into a new outfit and leave my office to resume their day. Not so with this little girl. She tearfully told me how her daddy was going to be mad that she got paint on her dress and sweater. I promised her I would "see what I could do" and sent her on her way in clean "borrowed" clothes.

Our school has a developmental preschool program. The students attend school Monday through Thursday. It being Friday, I realized there would be no students in the preschool class where they are equipped with a washer and dryer. On Fridays I often use these machines to wash blankets, and other items from my office that become soiled.

On this Friday, I took Mia's clothes to the washer, threw them in, and hoped for the best. To my amazement, every stain came out of the dress and sweater! I felt as if I was in a laundry detergent commercial as I admired the sparkling clean dress and sweater.

When Mia returned at the end of the day to change into her "ruined" dress, I presented her with the clean dress and sweater. I watched as her whole face lit up with joy over the clean dress. She was so happy that she threw her arms around me and gave me a big hug. She thanked me profusely and hugged me some more.

Every time I see Mia, she always stops by to say hi and she always rewards me with her bright smile. I learned that day that school nursing is so much more than bandages and ice packs. Sometimes the smallest gestures that have nothing to do with being a nurse, like just being there for a child, make all the difference in the world.

Dreams Do Come True

By Sharon L.H. Kelly, RN

I knew that I wanted to be a nurse by the tender age of seven. While other children were reading *Dick and Jane*, I laid on my mother's bed and poured over her nursing books. The pictures, and later the words, took me to the people and places that I wanted to be a part of one day. I decided on my specialty during first grade. After being sent to the school nurse for a knee abrasion I received during recess, my destiny was revealed to me as I limped into her office. I was so busy staring at all the wonderful items in her glass medical cabinet, I hardly even felt my wound being scrubbed and bandaged.

My nurse was a sight to behold. A no-nonsense woman, she wore a crisply starched white dress uniform. Her cap was snugly attached to her severely up done hair and her shoes gleamed with polish. She looked so wise and caring. Yes! I was going to be just like her. Forty years later, and after a varied and rewarding nursing career, my dream came true. I applied and was hired as the school nurse at my alma mater.

Recently, a first grader came into the health office sobbing. She had accidentally stepped in dog poop on her way to school. With utility gloves and a tongue depressor, I cleaned her sneakers, much to her relief and delight. And, as I cleaned, I noticed her as she looked around my office with the same wonderment I did, forty years ago.

Hang in There

By Janett Doile, RN

I accepted a school nursing position after I had been a nurse for 22 years. I also had been in the educational system helping as a special education paraprofessional. I thought that school nursing would be a perfect fit for me, matching my nursing knowledge and skills with my familiarity of the public education system. I felt I was a great candidate with my varied experiences. I had worked in hospitals, busy physicians' offices and my favorite, emergency rooms. I was confident that my skills and my love for children would make me a good school nurse.

Wow, my first year as a school nurse was a nightmare. I was hired in late September as the only nurse for a district of 1,600 students in five buildings. The nurse before me had left the April before without completing kindergarten round-up, so all of the kindergarten immunizations and health assessments had to be completed. The state audited my immunization records at the high school. We had a confirmed case of mumps just days before a basketball tournament with sixteen teams coming in to compete.

I went to work every morning telling myself, "You can do this," and drove home every afternoon asking myself, "What have you gotten yourself into?" I took work home. I went in early and stayed late. I called a friend who had been in school nursing for 20 years almost every day seeking answers and advice. I just kept telling myself I could do the job and continued to learn state policies and all other aspects of school nursing. I scrambled to get the vision, hearing, and scoliosis screenings completed. Then one day in April, I took stock and realized I had everything finished! The only work left to do was the day-to-day handling of health office requests.

My second year was much better. I learned how to manage the time and reports and I had time to enjoy the staff and students more. I almost did not return for my second year, but now in my 15th year of school nursing, I am so glad I stuck it out. It is a difficult job, and very few who are not in the field fully understand the requirements. However, the rewards from helping students and getting to know the young people are worth the demands.

The Wheelchair

By Wanda Fugett, RN, LSW, CHCQM-CM

It was the day before Christmas holidays were to begin. Even as students completed their semester tests, there seemed to be an excitement in the air. Adam was a very smart student who had a wonderful personality. He had more friends than almost anyone in the junior high school. He also had spina bifida.

I really enjoyed taking care of Adam during his visits to the nurse's office. He was always happy and smiling, in spite of the fact that he had some physical limitations from his illness.

His effervescent personality more than made up for any impairment that he had. Everyone in the school loved Adam, and his friends fought over who would get to wheel him to the nurse's office in his wheelchair, even though he was perfectly capable of doing it himself.

On this particular day, Adam and his friend were quiet. They usually came in laughing. Their faces looked sad and they seemed to be a little discouraged, which was very unusual. When I asked Adam what was wrong, he said, "My wheelchair is broken." He said that the chair would not roll straight. After some inspection, it was discovered that one of the wheels was loose.

A few months prior to this, a community member, Mr. Jones, had passed away. His wife, Mrs. Jones, attended the same church as our high school nurse. As Mrs. Jones went through her husband's belongings, she was not sure what to do with his wheelchair. She decided to offer it to our high school nurse, who was very happy to receive the gift. Because she already had a wheelchair at her school, the high school nurse thought the best thing to do was pass it along to the junior high campus.

I could not fix the broken wheel on Adam's wheelchair, and he needed to go back to class. Then I remembered the donated wheelchair, which was sitting in a closet. I pulled out the chair and brought it over to Adam. He was so excited! He would not have to try to walk to the remainder of his classes. Adam's friend Richie, who had been pushing the wheelchair, was equally excited.

Adam had already called his mother, who was concerned that Adam would have to walk to his classes the rest of the day. He was happy to call her again and report that a replacement wheelchair had been found! I was so thrilled when Adam left for class. He looked so good in the borrowed wheelchair being pushed by Richie.

I sent a thank you note to Mrs. Jones that day. I wanted to let her know what a difference she had made at the junior high school. I feel certain that this note helped Mrs. Jones in her grieving process, knowing that she and her late husband had helped a wonderful young man with spina bifida.

The life of a school nurse is a wonderful life. You never know what is going to happen next, or how it will all work out for the good of a student, and a person who is willing to help that student. I was grateful the day that I was able to furnish a donated wheelchair to a junior high school student who needed one.

Sight Reading

By Leisa Prasser, RN

I work in an elementary school that has second and third graders. Third grade vision screenings are a routine part of every school year, but occasionally a second grader needs a vision screening and is referred to me.

A typical second grader knows how to read and how to sound out words. This normally works just fine—*when reading!* One day, I was screening the vision of a little guy using a machine designed to check for visual acuity. I instructed him on where to place his head and asked him to read the letters by line number seven. He said he couldn't do it; so I asked him to read the line above, line six, which had bigger letters. He still couldn't do it. And so it went. I was finding it hard to believe that this young man's vision was really that bad! Was my testing faulty?

I finally said, "You can't see *any* of the letters?" To which he replied, "I can see the letters, but are they supposed to make words? I'm only in second grade and I might need help."

Problem solved! When I had instructed him to read the letters, he was *literally* trying to read. Since he was not able to sound out the "word" and make any sense of it, he just told me he couldn't read it. He actually screened at 20/20 vision in both eyes once I gave him better instructions.

I'd like to say this was a one-time incident, but it happened a few more times, even with some of the third graders. This prompted me to rephrase my wording to "Tell me what the letters are in line…" rather than reading "VRZKO." Just try to sound that out!

Charter School Nursing

By Michelle R. Simmons, RN, CSN, M. Ed

In recent years, the responsibilities of school nurses have evolved to meet the ever-changing needs of our students, families, and their communities. I have served as a school nurse in a research-based charter school for the last five years. Our charter school is located in an under-served community where traditional public school is failing. We are partnered with a local university that provides us with many resources that benefit our students and their families. Our school has also developed a partnership with our students' families and the community.

In our charter school, we take a holistic approach to educating our students. We strive to meet the needs of our students academically, socially, emotionally, and physically. We recognize that the child must be "whole" and have their needs met to succeed in a school environment. We are all aware that a hungry, anxious, or angry child will not thrive if these issues are not addressed. As the school nurse, I am a valuable member of the multi-disciplinary team that serves our students and their families. I advocate for our students and work closely with the school's social workers, psychology team, teachers, food manager, and administrators. By utilizing the team approach, we are better equipped to meet our goals. Many of our families are struggling and need additional support and services. As the nurse, many times the students, parents, and caregivers will confide in me, sharing the problems they are facing on any given day. Issues can range from being bullied to having no electricity in their home.

In addition to providing the usual state-mandated screenings each school year, I also coordinate extra services such as lead testing, mobile dental visits, bike helmet giveaways, gun safety and injury prevention programs, and diabetes and asthma education and support. I also provide strategies for health promotion and teach the importance of health maintenance. Gone are the days of just bandages and ice packs. We also often provide a sense of safety and stability in our students' lives. Many of our students and their families live very fragile, stressful lives—frequently relocating for various reasons. Our students spend many hours in school each week, so we can have a big influence on their daily lives. The school health office becomes their refuge for many reasons. Of course, our jobs are not without special rewards such as countless hugs, sweet hellos, and silly giggles. Sometimes, we receive specially designed notes and drawings from our grateful patients.

For years, there were public schools and private schools. Today, there are charter schools, cyber schools, and home schooling. Just as education has changed, so has school nursing, adapting to meet the ever-changing needs of our patient population. Many of today's school nurses have advanced degrees. Today, students' lives are much more complicated, requiring a comprehensive response to support academic success in school. School nurses now take a holistic approach to health and education through interdisciplinary collaboration.

I believe school nurses have truly evolved to become vital team members in the educational process. I am proud to be part of the profession of nursing, and even more proud of the specialty of school nursing. After all, we are working to educate the future citizens and leaders of our country.

Are You Serious?

By Janett Doile, RN

At my schools, I take the laundry home and wash it myself. This consists of a few towels, washcloths, sheets, and pillowcases every week. I use a top sheet and a pillowcase over a made bed so that it can easily be changed and a clean one applied. Therefore, I am rather protective of the use of the bed and only allow students on the clean sheets at my direction (I see no reason to do extra laundry).

One frequent flyer middle school student was continually coming in to the health office and plopping himself down on the bed with its clean sheets. Every time he did this, I asked him to please sit in a chair, not on the bed. Finally he got the idea and started sitting in a chair on his regular visits. One particular afternoon he walked in, obviously feeling pretty rough, and sat in a chair.

After taking his temperature and evaluating his complaints, I asked him if he would like to lie down on the bed while I called his mother. With his eyes wide, and a surprised look on his face he asked, "Are you serious, Mrs. Doile? I can really lay on the bed?"

The Mysterious Rash

By Brinda Friday, RN, BSN

Shortly after breakfast one morning, a special needs child was brought to the health center by his aide, who had a very worried look. The aide pointed out that this child had a bright pink "rash" on the inner aspect of one forearm.

At first glance, from several feet away, the nurse thought this rash did not look like any she had ever seen before. This was cause for alarm! However, upon closer assessment, the nurse detected the faint smell of strawberries on the child. Next, the nurse dampened a paper towel with warm water and proceeded to wash off a thin layer of strawberry jam. After a bit more cleaning, it was revealed that the child had perfectly normal skin, and the cause of the "rash" was most likely due to a strawberry pop tart eaten for breakfast!

Simple nursing assessment and intervention kept this student in school, instead of being sent home unnecessarily. Having a school nurse on-site protected the district from lost funding, and saved the child's parents from lost time.

A Cowgirl's Secret

By Debbra Y. House, RN – Author
Lynn Woods, RN - Co-Author
Barbara Cookerly, RN - Co-Author

We are three RN's working in a special needs (level 5) school located in a large metropolitan area. We have to think of unique ways to motivate our students to be independent in their personal care. This story was written to encourage our female students to be more aware of their personal hygiene. In addition, we can reverse the characters and use the story to motivate our male students.

There is a large farm in Texas called Friendly Barns. Mr. and Mrs. Happy are the owners of the farm. The Happy family has six children. They have five boys and one girl. All of the children help their parents run the farm. Each child has a special job they must do every day. The Happy family has lots of animals on their farm. They have horses, cows, pigs, and chickens. They also grow their own vegetables. They grow corn, potatoes, green beans, and carrots.

A normal day on the Happy's farm starts at 4:00 a.m. Mrs. Happy gets up first. She takes her shower and then brushes and flosses her teeth. Then she chooses the clothes she plans to wear for the day. Afterwards, she gets dressed, brushes her hair, and wakes up Mr. Happy. Mr. Happy gets up right away and starts his morning routine. Once he is finished, he heads out to the farm to start getting the animals ready for the day. Mrs. Happy then wakes up her daughter Lilly. Lilly is just nine years old and doesn't like to get up early. Mrs. Happy wakes Lilly up to get ready for school each day. Lilly loves to go to school to be with her friends; however, she has a big secret that she thinks no one knows about. Little does she know others are aware of her secret.

It was early Monday morning. Mrs. Happy had completed her morning routine and went to wake up Lilly for school.

"Lilly, it's time to get up," stated Mrs. Happy. Lilly did not move. She was sound asleep. Again, Mrs. Happy called out, "Lilly, it's time to get ready for school!"

She then called out to the boys to wake up. Mrs. Happy went downstairs to start breakfast for the family. Slowly but surely, the boys woke up and completed their morning routines. They each took a shower, brushed and flossed their teeth, and combed their hair. Lilly was still asleep in bed when her mother asked her to come down to breakfast. Lilly popped up out of the bed like bread popping out of a toaster. She ran into the bathroom to get ready.

Unfortunately, Lilly did not have enough time to complete her routine. So, she washed her face and brushed and flossed her teeth. She also brushed her hair and put on a nice outfit. The one thing she did not do was take a shower.

She came downstairs to eat her breakfast as usual. Her family commented on how nice her hair looked and how bright her smile was. They even noticed that her clothes looked nice. Lilly sat down to eat her breakfast, thinking to herself *No one knows that I didn't take a shower.* She smiled and felt good about the fact that she had a secret.

When Lilly came home from school that day, she asked her mother if she could watch her favorite cartoon after she finished her homework. Her mother said that would be okay. Lilly finished her homework and watched her favorite cartoon. Afterwards, she helped her mother prepare dinner.

Lilly liked helping her mother in the kitchen; however, she understood that working in the kitchen was a serious job, and she needed to be safe when picking up any dishes or kitchen supplies. Lilly also liked to ride her horse Cotton. She named him Cotton because he was so soft. On the weekends, Lilly worked in the garden with her mother planting vegetables and pulling up weeds.

The next school day arrived and Lilly was running late again. She popped out of bed like a piece of toast and dashed into the bathroom. *It happened again,* she thought to herself, *I don't have enough time to take a shower!*

So, she washed her face, brushed and flossed her teeth, and brushed her hair. Lilly knew her secret worked the last time, and she was sure it would work again. She went downstairs to eat breakfast as usual. Her family told her she looked nice.

However, when she got up to put her dishes in the sink, her mother commented that something smelled funny. Lilly quickly gathered her backpack and dashed out the door to get on the school bus. Once on the school bus, Lilly thought to herself *Did Mother notice I didn't take a shower today? I've only missed taking a shower for two days. I don't smell anything.* She looked out the bus window and started to daydream about coming home later and riding her horse Cotton.

Once Lilly arrived at school, she forgot all about the comment her mother made about a funny smell. She went to class and was glad to see her friends. After class they went to the cafeteria for lunch. While they were all laughing and talking, her friend Trish made a statement that shocked Lilly. Trish asked the girls, "Do you smell something funny?"

They all looked at each other in surprise.

"No, Trish," they said, "Do you smell something funny?"

Trish said, "Yes, and I wish the smell would go away. I noticed it yesterday when we were here, but I didn't say anything. It smells like somebody forgot to take a bath or shower."

The girls looked at each other and said, "It's not me."
Lilly left the table to go use the restroom. While in the restroom she began to cry. She thought to herself *I didn't know anyone could tell I didn't take a shower this morning.* She washed her hands and returned to the table with her friends. Again, Trish commented that the smell was back. The other girls told Trish, "It's not any of us. It must be someone at the other table next to us."

The girls returned to class. Lilly remained quiet for the rest of the day. When it was time to take the bus home, Lilly sat in the back of the bus with her head down. Her friends thought she didn't feel well so they left her alone. It was true, Lilly didn't feel well, but it was not because she felt sick. She was sad because she realized her friends had discovered her secret. She had refused to take a shower for two days and the smell could not be hidden. Lilly pledged to take a shower every day from that point on. The next day when her mother called her to get up for school, she jumped up like a piece of toast. This time, however, she went into the bathroom and took a shower before putting on her clothes.

Little Things

By Ann Ellington, RN

It was my first year as a school nurse. After 30 years in a clinical nursing setting, I was amazed and a little terrified by how much my students had to teach me.

Early one morning, I spotted him. You know the one: two-and-a-half feet tall, backpack bigger than him, walking with his head down as though his dog just died. I fell into step with him and we started chatting. We chatted about everything, and nothing, all at the same time.

I walked with him to his classroom, where he vanished into a sea of wiggling, tiny things. I continued to my office to start my day. That brief encounter lasted twice as long as the memory of it.

When I entered the school scene, the H1N1 and avian flu scare were hot on my heels. It became my mission to teach the students in my care how to wash their hands and cover their coughs and sneezes. I offered presentation after presentation on hygiene and coughing and sneezing etiquette.

Although school nurses do our jobs without expectation of receiving anything in return, it was such a blessing when one first grade class made "Thank You" booklets. Each child made a little book that included his or her favorite part of the presentation.

With tears in her eyes, the teacher said, "Look at Billy's book."

Puzzled, I searched my memory for Billy's face. As I searched the stack of books for his name, I had more luck locating the booklet. I thumbed through the pictures and the wobbly printing until I came to the "Thing I Liked Best" page. "Walking down the hall."

Stunned, I remembered the little boy with the backpack so many weeks ago. I recounted the incident to his teacher, and together, we realized that what took no thought at all on my part was imprinted on the heart of a child. What was an insignificant encounter for me was truly significant to him.

I keep Billy's booklet in my office, as a reminder that a second spent with a child is never insignificant.

OMG!

By Patricia VanHavermaat, BSN, RN, NCSN

The second year I was a school nurse, my "office" in the elementary school I served was a desk in the vault behind the school secretary's desk in the front office. I was intently working on immunization records, when all of a sudden I heard yelling and screaming as someone burst into the school office, "Where's the nurse? We need the nurse!" Of course, I jumped up and immediately came out of my vault expecting the absolute worst: a severed limb, a broken body part, or a gushing bleeding wound. I can tell you, my adrenaline was pumping and then some!

In the seconds, which seemed like hours, for my eyes and other senses to focus in on the scene, I discovered a small turtle had attached itself to the itty-bitty finger of one of my third graders. Not only did I not know what to do, I was terrified of turtles, snakes and all of the rest of that type of "pet." In two leaps I reached the screaming student and steered him into the closest room with a sink, his teacher following in hot pursuit. I turned on the cold water and thought *Well, if I put his finger under running cold water, the turtle will let go so as not to drown.*

That poor turtle endured gallons and gallons of water and still did not let go, nor did my student stop screaming. I shook the finger and finally, finally, the turtle fell off and circled (counter-clockwise by the way) in the sink. The teacher grabbed the turtle and ran back to her classroom. I assessed the injured finger and gave the appropriate treatment along with a good measure of TLC as well as a strong dose of "What the heck were you thinking, putting your finger in the turtle's mouth?!" (Well, maybe not in those exact words, but you get the gist).

The finger was fine, the turtle lived to go home and never attended school again, and the nurse managed to survive a run-in with a turtle. I did do some follow-up research about how to dislodge a turtle from a digit; you squeeze its jaws together, and it will open its mouth. Go figure. To this very day, after all of these years, I am so grateful I did not know that then, as I am not sure I could have touched the turtle. As glad as I am that the turtle did not drown, I am even happier that the water eventually worked. Needless to say, the whole turtle-at-school incident became a teaching moment about the diseases a turtle can carry and pass on. And, yes, I did share how to get a turtle's mouth open!

May I Please Have a Peppermint?

By Frances Harmon, RN, BSN, PHN

Dear Dad,

Finally! Finally I am all caught up with my studies and have not two, not three, but *five* whole days off in a row! At last I can write you back and update you on everything that has been happening.

Let's see…where did I leave you last?

Oh yes! Last spring…

As you know, last spring I was taking an audiology course which is another class required before I can obtain my school nurse credential. Yes, it would have been much simpler had I just studied the bits and pieces that make up the ear, but the course demanded much more than that. We had to understand the various causes of hearing loss, the various methods of testing for hearing loss, and how to interpret the tests, among other things.

How right you were to take my ear infections seriously, Dad! When I was growing up, I wonder if you knew just how many complications could occur. When I was a little girl, all I really understood about ear infections was that they hurt. I had no idea that multiple ear infections could permanently damage the ear. What I now find frightening is how many things can cause permanent hearing loss—even certain medications can impact a child's hearing! After the class was completed, those of us who managed to pass the course were able to apply for our audiology technician certification.

And can we talk about noise pollution for a minute? I think I am beginning to sound like you when it comes to loud music. I remember how you hated to hear radios blasting music from the cars next to you on the freeway. At the time, we were only concerned that the driver wouldn't be able to hear an approaching emergency vehicle's siren, but as I've learned this semester, the consequences are far more serious.

The other day, my husband and I went to a movie. The sound was cranked up so loud that it made my seat vibrate! By the time I left the theater, I couldn't hear what Doug was saying and he was standing right next to me. If a loud two-hour movie could have such a dire effect on my hearing, I dread thinking about the long-term damage from the ear buds everyone uses to hear their music. I am sure that parents and children do not realize that they should limit exposure to their tunes if they decide to keep the volume on high.

From what I've read, I now know that 60 dB is the sound of a typical conversation, 85 dB is the sound of traffic, and 90 dB is the sound of a loud hairdryer. Using an mp3 player or similar device at peak volume is 115 dB, which is 5dB less than a jackhammer. A person only has to listen to their device at peak volume for *two hours a day* before they experience *permanent* hearing damage.

I am sure I don't have to convince you to believe that a person using ear buds with music blaring at full volume can cause hearing damage by listening to the thing for more than *five minutes a day!* But it is hard to convince the children or their parents that this is a serious problem, that is until I catch the children saying, "Huh?!" or "What?" when their parent is speaking to them.

Ah, kids…what can you do? Sadly, some lessons they will only allow themselves to learn the hard way.

Anyway, that was last semester. You will never believe what happened this semester.

This semester I began the mentor program. School nurse candidates are assigned to mentors who are already working within the school systems. Because I know you will never guess where I was assigned, I will just tell you. *I was assigned to my old elementary school!* And, as if that were not uncanny enough, my mentor is *Nurse Judge!* She has been there since the school opened 51 years ago, and here I am working by her side. I think she has found the secret of youth because she is still as sharp as a tack and has one heck of an incredible memory. She knows every child's name that attends the school, she knows their parents' and grandparents' names and, in many cases, she even took care of the parents and grandparents! At this point, she is on her fourth generation of students.

My first orientation day was interesting. After I got over the shock of finding out that Mrs. Judge was my mentor—and, truly, I couldn't have asked for a more experienced or better mentor—I heard a strange noise. It sort of sounded like hail hitting the roof of an old metal shed, but the sound seemed to increase and there wasn't a cloud in the sky. Mrs. Judge didn't even seem to notice the sound. I thought it was because her hearing wasn't quite as good as it was 51 years ago, but I soon found out I was wrong about that!

Just as I was about to ask her what was causing the noise, at least 15 children ranging from early fifth to eighth grade appeared in the doorway. This was the source of the sound. All of them seemed to be yelling something. All I could understand was "Can I have…" The rest made no sense at all.

Mrs. Judge stopped restocking her bandages and slowly turned. As if by magic, all the children stopped and were still. Then she said, "What do you say?"

She raised her hand as if to direct a finally trained orchestra, the children asked in perfect unison, "Can we please have a peppermint?"

"Yes, you may have a peppermint, but only one! Now remember, when you say *'can'* I have a peppermint, you are asking me if you are *capable* of having a peppermint. When you use the word *'may'* you are asking permission! Now go and play and *be careful!* You there, Alex! How many times do I have to tell you to tie that shoe? One of these days you will trip and fall and break your arm!"

They all thanked her as they formed a line for the jar of peppermints. It was then that I noticed the inscription on the jar that read, "'May I please have a peppermint?' love the class of '79." Behind the container hung a picture of Mrs. Judge sitting at her desk holding the jar, looking exhausted but happy.

As you read this, I wonder whether you are as confused about the whole peppermint thing as I was. I had to ask her what was with the peppermint jar. Once she explained things, it all made perfect sense.

As you know, mint and ginger both help soothe an upset stomach. When the children have upset stomachs, she will have them try a peppermint to see if it will calm their stomachaches. She used to have ginger ale but it was just too hard to keep in the office. The peppermints were much easier to keep in stock. She also explained to me that she will only allow the children to have one peppermint a day because any more than that and it is just a candy. Whether it was the mint itself that helped to soothe the child's stomach, or it was the feeling that they were loved and tended to that did its magic, Mrs. Judge said it worked about 98% of the time. Needless to say, this is not a little trick they teach you in college.

My college courses also failed to warn me about the "Dear Parent" letters I found myself typing under the watchful eye of Mrs. Judge. I had my first taste of that my third week into the new school year. *"Dear Parents: It has come to our attention that several children have lice."* The following week, I found myself typing another letter *"Dear Parents: Whooping cough has reached epidemic levels"* then another letter, *"Dear Parents: One of our older students seems to have chicken pox."* The list of "Dear Parent" letters seemed to go on and on. After having a spotless record for 50 years, I can only blame the "Dear Parent" letters on the spirits of school nurses past having great fun at my expense!

My orientation continued through recess. I saw countless skinned knees, bloody noses, twisted ankles, and heads battered by tetherballs. Additionally, I treated stomachs that had gotten in the way of dodgeballs and fingers jammed by basketballs. There were a few bees that managed to lose their stingers in children and one child even had a seizure. Through it all, Mrs. Judge listened calmly as sobbing children told her the cause of their injuries. As she treated and soothed each child, it was as if a spell came over them and, before they knew it, they were laughing and telling Mrs. Judge the latest knock-knock joke.

Yes, we bandaged sprained ankles, scraped away stingers, treated bloody noses, administered to an asthma attack, and tended to a seizure, but these matters were only a miniscule part of what school nurses do to earn their keep. Through it all, I recalled what my first nursing instructor told us. As we stood frozen in fear with the thought of taking care of our very first patient, she reminded us, "I can train a chimp to do *things*. Doing *things* isn't what makes you a nurse. What makes you a nurse is when you are able to understand *why* you do these things!"

So, while I learned that asphalt and balls always win their battle against any body part, and that tetherball and dodgeball are really insanely dangerous games, I also learned that the role of the school nurse goes far beyond simply putting bandages on wounds or ice on sprained ankles. You have to learn to listen and be able to put a bandage on hearts, not just knees. You are a teacher and a mentor. You are a safe and friendly ear, and you are a source of unconditional love. These are things you cannot be trained to do. These are things you are born to do.

When I walked on the campus that morning, I thought nothing had changed since my days there as a student. The tetherball and dodgeball areas were where I remembered them. The volleyball courts were in the same place as well. Even the old eye chart in Mrs. Judge's office was the same as I remembered it over twenty years ago. However, after spending a day with Mrs. Judge, I left the campus and noticed slight changes.

The poles that held the basketball hoops were now padded, the balls the children played with were no longer hard leather balls, but were now of softer, gentler material. The school now has a program for kindergarteners and early-5's thanks to Mrs. Judge developing the curriculum and raising money to build the classrooms. Many of the children on the playground that wore glasses did so because they had been screened by Mrs. Judge. As I left the campus, I could see her loving touch everywhere I looked.

I am eager to help and learn from Mrs. Judge as we begin our vision and hearing screening tests after the Thanksgiving holiday. We will be starting our screenings a bit later than most schools, but we have to wait our turn to borrow the equipment. I have no doubt that Mrs. Judge will be able to add to what I learned from the audiology class. I am sure she will be able to put into better perspective the *why* and not just the *how* of the screenings.

Oh and of course, before I left her office, I asked Mrs. Judge for a peppermint. They really do seem to soothe both a person's body and mind!

I know I will have so much more to share with you but, for now, I will give your eyes a rest. I love you and miss you.

Yours,
Frances

Just a Worm!

By Patricia Hamilton, RN

It was the end of the day and my aide and I were wrapping things up in the nurse's office. Our students were lining up across the hall to go home. Suddenly, we heard a teacher yell, "Student down—head injury!"

Immediately, my aide and I grabbed gloves and ran across the hall to assist the student.

When we arrived, little "Harry Potter" was lying flat on his back, with both hands behind his head. The teacher reported that another student accidentally pushed him to the floor.

I identified myself and told him we were there to help. Without moving him, I began a visual assessment. He was crying, but alert. He knew his name and where he was.

I gently removed his glasses for safety, and to assess his pupils. So far, so good!

Still lying on his back, I asked him to wiggle his toes. He could! So far, so good!

My next thought was that I needed to support his head and neck, and roll him on his side to assess the back of his head. Meanwhile, my little boy wizard look-alike was still holding his head in his hands.

I slowly and gently began to roll him. No bleeding noted. So far, so good!

Then, I looked in the palm of his little hand and—oh my goodness! Inside of his hand was some kind of tan/pinkish matter! My first thought was...BRAIN!

I carefully removed the matter from his hand. It was mushy and about two inches long. Oh my gosh—it was a little tan rubber worm!

I immediately handed the worm to my assistant, picked up "Harry Potter," and moved him into the nurse's office to wait for mom's arrival.

Mom arrived! SO FAR, SO GOOD!

What's in the Cup?

By Connie Trent, RN, BSN

I work in the primary department of our school. This means I care for Pre-K, kindergarten, first grade, and special education students. I knew this would be a rough morning. The time change from daylight savings time had occurred the previous weekend, and it always affected our young students. In the first half hour of school, I had kids coming in my office right off the bus with earaches, colds, and even vomiting.

In addition to those illnesses, the insulin pump of one of my diabetic students began sounding an alarm, which read "not primed." A feeding tube site on another student had something coming out of it!

When I thought the morning couldn't get any crazier, a substitute teacher called me to report that a child just handed her a cup partially filled with urine. Apparently the child's mother told her to give it to the teacher. It was a specimen cup—with no lid! I told the teacher I had a few other issues to handle, but I would call the student's mother, and then walk down to the classroom to retrieve the cup.

When things calmed down a bit, I called Mom to ask about the cup, and why her daughter presented it to the teacher. She said, "Oh yes, we have to get a urine sample to see if she has an infection. We forgot to get it over the weekend."

"Where is the lid?" I asked.

The mother indicated it was in her daughter's book bag—of course! I grabbed a pair of gloves and went to the classroom.

The substitute teacher said she had placed the urine sample on the bathroom sink. I opened the door, and another child was in there. She immediately said, "I didn't touch it," (so you know she did).

The cup now had a lid on it, and it was *full!* I asked the teacher about all the paper towels around the cup. She looked at the cup and said, "It was only half full when the child brought it to me."

The question became: what *else* was in the cup? Water? Soap? Another urine specimen from another child? I called the student's mother back and told her the specimen had been contaminated. She would have to get another cup from the doctor and do it again—**at home.** Whew! What a morning!

VI.

Humorous Stories

*"Listening to my students' stories
is one of the best things
about being a school nurse."*

–Carol A. Tucker, RN, BSN

I'll Have the Same

By Leisa Prasser, RN

It had been a really long day at the elementary school, one of those when you think *It's never going to end!* A stomach virus had hit our school population with a vengeance. The morning had been so quiet, but by lunchtime the clinic was full of children. Two students were occupying the two beds and others were lined up to see me. Some had stomach cramps; others had already vomited in other locations of the school. Yuck!

Child number three came into the clinic complaining of a headache. Well, that was different. Numbers one and two had the stomach bug. I took number three's temperature and he did not have a fever. Wanting to scoot at least one out of the clinic, I quickly gave him some acetaminophen. Parents of our students sign for permission for this to be given at school. He readily took the medicine and then stood by my desk as I wrote a note to his parent informing about the medication administration. He had been extremely quiet the whole time. I was halfway through my note writing, when—you guessed it—number three threw up! The vomit ended up on my desk, the floor, my shoes, and on vision screening forms that were completed and ready to be filed. He had not mentioned once that he had an upset stomach!

Three students were standing outside the clinic door waiting to see me. When I asked the next student why he was here, he jerked his thumb up and motioned toward the other kids, "Same as them!"

I asked, "What do you mean 'same as them'?"

He then replied, "I'm here trying to throw up and I can't, just like them!"

It was extremely hard to maintain my composure, but I managed a straight face and told him, "There will be NO *trying* to throw up!" The other adults in the office area had a really good laugh when they overheard the conversation.

Friends Don't Let Friends Eat Boogers

By Dena Weeks, LVN

On a boring old day in January, three boys dared each other during lunch. One boy licked his hot dog, put it on his shoe, and dared his friend to eat it. And the friend did! Not to be outdone, a third friend picked his booger and gave it to the hot dog eater, daring him. Well, that was too much and the hot dog eater got sick before eating the booger (thank goodness). All three boys were sent to the office for misbehavior.

As the teacher and assistant principal told me the story, I laughed out loud. They asked if I would do a little lecture on germs and maturity. The boys had to have heard me laughing, so I began by telling them that I thought the assistant principal was telling me about a funny movie when she said, "No, it was three of our 4th graders." I told them in a silly movie or cartoon this might be humorous, but in real life this was NOT funny and proceeded to read the riot act.

I explained that germs would make them sick and how important it was to never touch someone else's spit, snot, blood, pee, or poo (juvenile snickers at the latter). I told them that to dare someone was to be a bully. Too many accidents and even deaths started out as just a dare. Never dare someone and NEVER take a dare. Real men don't take dares. They believe that a dare is stupid and won't do it.

I went on to tell them that they were old enough to know better. The assistant principal added the burden that as 4th graders, they were supposed to set an example for the younger students. The boys were contrite and seemed to understand how serious the situation was. How I kept a straight face, I will never know, but I was tough. The assistant principal reminded them that everyone makes mistakes and this was theirs. She admonished them not to let this kind of thing happen again. After the boys went back to class the whole office staff laughed for the rest of the day.

You can pick your friends...you can pick your nose...but you can't pick your friend's nose...and never eat boogers... neither yours nor your friend's...and finally...friends don't let friends eat boogers.

A Peppery Encounter

By Colleen Henson, RN, CSN

With so many students in and out of the health room for various and assorted illnesses, injuries, and problems, I have seen my fair share of significant issues. However, it's the ones that, after the issue has been resolved, make me laugh and keep everything in perspective that I value the most. One such issue occurred on an otherwise "normal" day a few years ago in the high school I serve.

A young man, I'll call him John, came flying into the health room past the lineup of usual upset stomachs, nosebleeds, and menstrual cramps that were waiting for their turn to be seen. I just knew this had to be a real emergency, and I was ready to grab my portable emergency kit and wheelchair to respond to wherever this young man indicated that I was needed. However, I quickly learned that it was HE who needed my attention as he continued to move anxiously about the health room.

"Do you have anything for burning?" John asked, with tears welling up in his eyes.

I thought that he must be having some kind of epigastric disturbance and quickly shoved a waste can towards him, believing that he was experiencing the latest stomach virus that was plaguing our students.

"No," he quickly interjected, "I mean…my skin is burning."

Having seen numerous students in the health room for welding accidents or chemistry mishaps, I knew I needed to assess the injured area to determine the best course of treatment to alleviate the burning. I then asked the next obvious question, "Where is your skin burning?" Still prancing around the room, he looked sheepishly towards me and began to wince. Whispering, so as not to draw any further attention or embarrass himself any further, he said, "It's my privates." I immediately emptied the room, sending the majority of students across the hall to the attendance office so that I could have more privacy with John and determine the next steps that should be taken. He relayed a story that I'd never heard before and have not heard since.

He began the saga: "My friend brought in some REALLY hot, hot peppers and dared some of us at the lunch table to try some. I ate a little of one, and it burned really bad. But then I went to the restroom, and now I feel like I'm on fire!" The oil residue from the pepper remained on John's hand, and, of course, he didn't wash his hands *before* using the rest room. The pepper's oil had made its way to an area that it should never be. I quickly tried to research antidotes on the internet only to find that the affected area should be cleansed with soap and water until the burning sensation stops. I gave John a disposable washcloth and directed him to a closed-off room with a sink and soap. As John continued to try to relieve the burning pain, I questioned him through the closed door as to his status.

"It's not working very well," he cried, his voice cracking with the discomfort.

While John was attempting to wash away the cause of his pain, I walked across the hall to the principal's office to see how the other students were doing. The wonderful secretarial staff had attended to the majority of the students' needs, so I began telling one of the secretaries the saga that had occurred across the hall without revealing who the student was.

"Oh," Sue began, "that must have been a habañero pepper. There were several students that were talking about that earlier."

I explained that the burning and discomfort that the student was feeling was not from eating the pepper, but rather from a much more personal encounter with the pepper's oil.

"Wow! That happened to my husband not very long ago. He had to pour milk over himself to get the burning to stop."

Hearing that, I quickly ran from the attendance office down to the school cafeteria to request a carton of milk. Not too sure of the logistics of how John would try this remedy, I ran the carton of milk back to the health room.

"How's it going in there, John?" I asked.

"Not very well," John retorted with a quivering voice.

"Well, I know it sounds a little odd, but I may have something that will help. Open the door and I'll hand it to you."

After a few moments, the door cracked open and John, red-faced and sweating, took the milk carton from me. The look on his face suggested that he might have thought I was crazy.

"Whatever way you want to try to work it out, if you are able to get milk on the affected area, it should relieve the burning."

After about 5 minutes, John came out of the secluded room looking wilted, but relaxed.

"It worked!" he exclaimed, almost breathless.

After another 15 minutes of rest on a cot, John returned to class, and did not return to the nurses' office again that day. I'm not sure if it was because he truly did not experience any further problems, or if he was now too embarrassed to return to see me again.

We all have days when we think *Why am I here?* Incidents like the one I had with John make me realize at the end of the day there are always needs for our students that we can never predict. It truly helps to keep things in perspective daily and to laugh a little when all returns to normal.

You Want to Look at What?

By Tina Clark, RN, BSN

Just when you think students are not listening, a child will say something to prove you wrong.

I have been a school nurse for thirteen years in the same building of kindergarten through fifth graders. One year I was working with a student nurse during her public health rotation. She was working hard and really connecting with the young students. A young man came in the office complaining of a sore throat. The student nurse jumped in to do an assessment. No fever, no congestion noted, no complaints of a stomachache. The student nurse and I were going to look at the patient's throat. Penlight ready, tongue depressor in hand, she asked the patient to open up to look at his throat. He suddenly ducked, avoided us, and yelled, "You aren't going to touch my uvula with that are you?"

The student nurse and I were stunned that a student in second grade would remember they have a uvula, and its location! So when you think your students are not listening in health class or during opportunities to educate, I know for a fact one student is listening.

This second grader could not leave the nurse's office fast enough. The student nurse and I could not keep from giggling much longer.

I truly enjoy my job as a school nurse.

The Nurse Can Fix It

By Dena Weeks, LVN

Oh, why did I leave my camera at home?

Just as I was leaving for my lunch break one day, a frustrated teacher brought in a student, who had obviously caused the frustration. Attached to the boy was a white laundry basket made of sturdy plastic and, of course, it boasted very...small... holes. The third grader had his index, middle, and ring fingers in three of the very...tiny...small...holes. Mrs. Frustrated said, "I know it's your lunch time, but I thought maybe you had some petroleum jelly, or something to help his fingers slip out."

The student's index and ring fingers were small enough to slip out of the very...teeny...tiny...small...holes, but the middle finger was too big and had already started to swell. I liberally applied petroleum jelly to his middle finger hoping that the finger would slip out. **It didn't work.** I put ice on his finger hoping to reduce the swelling. **It didn't work.** I elevated his hand above his head hoping to reduce the swelling. **It didn't work.** The finger was securely stuck in the very...minute... teeny...tiny...small...hole.

"Why did you do this?" I exclaimed.

The boy answered, "Well, I thought that they would come out if they went in." This is perfect logic for an eight year old. Then he told me how his classmate started to put his fingers in but they wouldn't fit. So, he did it and they got stuck.

With no other option, I decided to cut the plastic basket. The basket was surprisingly sturdy, and regular scissors were useless. Fortunately, I have a toolbox, which includes a pair of small wire cutters. They would be the perfect tool to safely cut sturdy plastic without harming human fingers.

Unfortunately, the principal knew where my toolbox was located and had borrowed my wire cutters. Since the principal was off campus at a meeting, I couldn't ask him where they were. After frantic searching for wire cutters or tin snips or any tool strong enough to cut heavy plastic, the librarian saved the day. She also had a toolbox, which included a pair of wire cutters.

I carefully snipped at the plastic from one very... extremely...minute...teeny...tiny...small...hole to the very... extraordinarily...extremely...minute...teeny...tiny...small... hole in which the finger was securely and firmly wedged. I then bent the cut plastic and the student was able to remove his finger.

The child was fine (we didn't have to amputate his finger). The basket was broken. I told the librarian to hide her toolbox from the principal.

Moral of this story: don't stick your fingers where they don't belong.

I Want MY Quarter Back

By Kathy Nyalka, RN

It was a very uneventful day at school until the music teacher rushed Sally into the nurse's office, exclaiming, "She swallowed a quarter!" Sally was a beautiful girl with dark hair and impressive eyes. I saw Sally often, and knew that her family life was difficult. Her mother left, and she was being raised by her father and grandparents.

Sally was a very nervous person, always fidgeting and biting her nails. The teacher explained that another student had dropped a quarter during class. Sally picked it up and put it in her mouth! Of course, she accidentally swallowed the quarter. She started choking, the teacher tried to do the Heimlich maneuver on her, and when that did not work, he rushed her to my office.

I asked Sally "Why did you put the quarter in your mouth?" She was unable to answer me. I realized she had a partial airway obstruction. I called her emergency contacts, but no one was available to come for her. I looked at Sally again. The quarter needed to come out—which meant I needed to call for emergency care. As I reached for the phone to dial 9-1-1, Sally had to throw up. Guess what she threw up: the quarter!

I fished the quarter out of the wastebasket, and gave it a thorough cleaning. I then attempted to call her family again—this time her grandmother was available to pick her up. When her grandmother arrived, I instructed her to seek medical advice, and handed the quarter back to Sally.

Sally returned to school the next day, and while in music class, the student who had dropped the quarter asked for it back. Believe it or not, she returned the quarter to the student who had dropped it!

New Treatment for Respiratory Infection

By Dena Weeks, LVN

Was this just another manic Monday or a humorous day in the life of a school nurse? It was a rainy, dreary, Monday in February, the middle of flu season, and the nurse needed to leave campus early to attend a mandatory meeting.

Mondays are always busy, especially during cold and flu season. Several students had been sent home with symptoms of fever, sore throat, and cough on that particular day. Just as the nurse was leaving for her meeting, a first grader came to the clinic with a horrible cough. The little boy had a history of asthma so the nurse listened to his lungs. She called the child's father and explained that while he had no fever, his lungs sounded serious and urged the father to take the boy to the doctor. The father arrived quickly, and he and his son left school, and the nurse left for the meeting.

The next morning, the little boy came back to the clinic to report about his afternoon. According to the 6-year-old, he went to the Emergency Day Care and got medicine for the squirts. He said that his stomach hurt and showed the nurse that under his ribcage was sore. Puzzled, the nurse asked if he had diarrhea, too. The child said he didn't know but his stomach hurt and he still had the cough. Needing clarification, the nurse called the boy's father. She told the father what the son had reported. Laughing, the father explained that the doctor's office was booked and referred them to the Emergency Care Center. His son was given a liquid medicine that was squirted into his mouth for a respiratory infection.

The Fly

By Patricia VanHavermaat, BSN, RN, NCSN

My middle school nurse's office used to face the courtyard. The door opened to the outside. In hot weather before the air conditioners were turned on, I would often prop the door open to get some fresh air.

One afternoon, as I was working at my desk with the door open, I heard feet running down the sidewalk. I braced myself for the worst, wondering what emergency situation I was about to be summoned to!

A student burst through my door saying, "I swallowed a fly! I swallowed a fly!" Her eyes were as big as saucers and she was breathless. Without thinking I asked, "Did it taste like chicken?" She stopped cold and immediately said, "Oh Nurse Trish" and burst out laughing, as did I. Along with rinsing her mouth out and giving her a drink of water, my unplanned words were 'the best medicine' I could have given this young lady. School nurses just seem to be blessed with the innate ability to do what is needed, emergency or not!

Another Battle in the War on Childhood Obesity

By Carol A. Tucker, RN, BSN

Our elementary speech teacher came in to the school nurse office one day, full of laughter. As soon as she caught her breath, she explained that she had a story to share. She was working with a student who said he had something to tell her from the news. She sensed his serious tone.

The student asked her if she knew that Sesame Street was going to change Cookie Monster's name. She asked if he knew why they were going to change his name or what his new name would be. The little boy shrugged his shoulders, and said he did not know what the new name would be. He continued to explain, "Well, they're changing it because he's not going to just eat cookies anymore. He's going to eat healthy foods like fruits and vegetables." The speech teacher responded that would be a good idea. The student replied, "Yeah, they're doing it to get rid of childhood obedience." At this, the teacher had to end her session with the student because she was laughing so hard.

Our children try so hard to understand what's going on in the world around them, but often their impressions take on new interpretations as they share with others. Listening to my students' stories is one of the best things about being a school nurse.

And the Oscar Goes to...

By Elizabeth Cabrera, RN

I became a registered nurse at the age of 48. This in and of itself was a dream come true, especially when I received the phone call with the job offer I had always wanted: elementary school nurse. I was so gung ho that I had finally accomplished my dream. Had my children still been in grade school, it would have been perfect.

My first year as a school nurse proved to be very interesting. As a mother of four, I have developed eyes in the back of my head, the hearing of an eagle, and I know every trick in the book. You had to wake up pretty early to put one over on this ol' gal. Pretty soon, I earned the reputation of being a "tough nurse." I wouldn't let children slide by as easily as the previous nurse had. The students tried turning on the tears, faking a dry cough, limping, saying they had just thrown up, yet their breath smelled like candy. CSI had nothing on this nurse. Not only was I a mother of four creative and intelligent actors and actresses, I had completed a double major and graduated with a bachelor's degree in Social Psychology. I was strutting around this school as the "baddest" nurse in town. I thought I had seen and heard it all. Until Xavier.

It was lunchtime, with a playground full of kindergartners playing rambunctiously—monkey bars full of little hands with legs waving in the air—but one student was not among them. I received a call on the radio, "Nurse! Nurse! Child down by the cafeteria doors!" My heart immediately began pumping, as my not-so-petite (I deem it pleasantly plump) frame began racing down the hall. I arrived on the scene to find the playground monitor stooped over a small boy. The boy was laying on the concrete walkway, and appeared to be non-responsive.

I began my assessment, checking his airway, breathing, and circulation. All present. I tried to elicit a response by yelling "Xavier—Xavier!" No response. I picked up the limp child and, looking like the Pillsbury Doughboy™ carrying a rag doll, ran to my office. The playground monitor followed.

I set Xavier onto the examination table. His body remained frail, limp, and lifeless. I checked his pulse and breathing again—still normal. I feared I might have to place my first emergency call. I tried to wake him once more by patting his face, and calling out "Xavier? Xavier, can you hear me?! Xavier!"

I felt that it was time—I had to call 9-1-1. Then I realized that I forgot to check for pupil reaction. I quickly found my penlight and attempted to check his eyes. It was then that I noticed Xavier was making an effort to keep his eyelids closed. That little booger! Not missing a beat, I told the playground monitor, "Quick—I know what we need to do! Help me stand him up and get him naked."

The volunteer quickly looked at me with alarm—I gave her a wink as we continued to hold up his listless body. As I started to grab his belt buckle, Xavier suddenly sprang to life, with the most embarrassed "you caught me" look upon his face. I was floored! I thought my children were the best of the best until Xavier.

I then gave him a stern lecture and sent him back to class. Returning to my office, I called his mother to report the day's events. Apparently this was normal behavior, and she suggested that next time I threaten to give him a shot if he acted up again. Boy oh boy was I livid.

Of course, I had no way of knowing that I hadn't seen everything yet. I later realized that he deserved an Oscar for his star performance! I live to learn, and look forward to my next great adventure as a school nurse.

Pillsbury Doughboy is a registered trademark of General Mills, Inc. and is used with permission.

MacGILL
DISCOUNT MEDICAL AND SCHOOL NURSE SUPPLIES

MacGill was established as a medical supply company in 1904, and school nurses became our central focus in 1981. Today, school nurses account for more than 95 percent of our business. Our primary objective is to satisfy the medical supply needs of school nurses at the lowest possible price. We have enjoyed working with you over the years and would like to express our deepest gratitude for your loyal patronage.

The majority of items in the MacGill Discount Medical and School Nurse Supplies Catalog are priced significantly lower than our competitors. Compare prices between catalogs to discover the great savings with MacGill.

For a free copy of the latest catalog, please visit us online at www.macgill.com, send an e-mail to macgill@macgill.com, or call toll-free 1-800-323-2841.